MASTERING the ABCs of EXCELLENT WRITING

MASTERING the ABCs of EXCELLENT WRITING

Creating Vivid and Colorful Stories
that Readers Want to Read

RANDY C. DOCKENS
ROBERT IRVIN

MASTERING the ABCs of EXCELLENT WRITING: Creating Vivid and Colorful Stories that Readers Want to Read

©2023 Randy C. Dockens and Robert Irvin

All rights reserved. No part of this book may be reproduced or transmitted in any form or by any means, electronic or mechanical, including photocopying, recording or by any information storage and retrieval system, without permission in writing from the copyright owner.

Published by Quill & Quotation Press, Franklin, Tennessee

Cover and Interior Design by Suzanne Lawing

Printed in the United States of America
ISBN 979-8-9902629-0-4

All quotes from famous authors placed at the beginning of each chapter are taken from Freewrite: https://getfreewrite.com/blogs/writing-success/55-motivational-writing-quotes.

PREFACE

How This Book Can Help You

(As They Say: Please Don't Skip This Section; You Might Miss Something Important)

There are many books on writing, so why another?

What I (Randy) discovered as I began my writing journey was that knowing the rules and applying the rules are not necessarily the same thing. You've heard the expression: *rules are made to be broken*. Well, that is certainly true when writing a book. I wish someone had told me this truth in the beginning.

In this book we aim to tell you some important rules, but just as importantly, we aim to tell you when they can be—gently—broken.

The other thing missing from so many books on writing is *you*. You are what makes your stories, your writing, unique from all others. We want you to include you in your writing. So we're giving you what we (Randy as an author, and Bob as an editor, writer, and author) wished we had known and understood when we started our writing and editing journeys.

Much of what we say in this book will benefit fiction writers, but almost all aspects can benefit nonfiction writers as well. So be aware of this throughout: as we write, we can't continually move back and forth from the base of fiction or nonfiction writing. The voice in this book may tend toward fiction, since that is what many people who aspire to write look to accomplish with their first, or early, works. But the engagements here will work across all types of writing.

If you master everything in this book, will you have a bestseller and start grossing a six-figure income from your books? Unfortunately, no one can guarantee that, and in truth, the answer is likely no. (Books of material have been written on this topic, and a common theory is that it takes seven published books before you begin to make some solid money. *That* belief, though, is just a rule of thumb, and maybe that rule also is meant to be broken—or at least bent some—by you.)

If you want to be classified as a good writer and want those who read your work to enjoy your books, we think this two-book series can help. While there are a lot of science and writing techniques that go into a good piece of literature, there is an art element that is every bit as much a part of its creation. That's why no two authors produce identical works. You can give two authors the same story outline and come away with two extremely different pieces of literature that have different twists and may even go in entirely different directions.

The science of the writing, like most of what is in this book, is a key part of that output, but so is the individual creativity of the mind of the author. This book will help you with the first part—and hopefully spur you a bit onward with the second. Your imagination, however, is truly the only thing that can help or limit you with that second aspect. Our aim is to assist you with the second part with the ideas in this book. We want this book to help inspire your creativity. These two aspects of writing—given care, diligence, and passion—together will make you an unstoppable force.

Also, though we think this book is a good size—not too lean, not too heavy, but just right—this work cannot contain everything you need to know or will need to learn. Yet it will get you started on the right foot and, we think, save you a great deal of time and effort in what you need to know to produce a quality piece of literature from the outset.

We also provide three cautions, or encouragements, in this introduction.

First, a frequent characteristic of avid readers is they often read with an eye to *finishing* a book. We just want to get to the end so we can add it to our completed reading list. (Which is a good thing!) But don't rush through this. And don't figure the last chapters are mere filler, or that the importance of the material somehow wanes toward the end, particularly because the letters *U, V, X, Y,* and *Z* seem like filler by their very nature (even though a talented Scrabble player knows just how valuable those letters can be!). It's the same thing with this book. We think some of our best encouragement comes in, well, all twenty-six chapters, including those lesser-used-lettered ones at the end.

This second point may seem a bit counterintuitive to the one just mentioned, though it's really not. You want to write. And want to do so well. So, you think you'll read this book in its entirety, and digest everything as close to perfectly as you can before you start writing. Or you think you'll read two other excellent books on writing you've chosen, and this one, before starting to write. Our encouragement: don't do that! Read a bit of this work, and let it help. But start writing! You're going to be perfecting the craft of writing your entire life. (We certainly are.) Just start. You'll keep learning and adding to your knowledge by reading companion books like this as you go. (But yes, also, please keep reading this book while you are writing, and do finish it.)

Third: yes, there is a logicality to this book with its organization and the section headers we've put together. We think it can make sense to read it straight through at the pace you've chosen. But if you want to skip around to help certain aspects of your writing, then do! Skip, skip, skip away! Find areas you're particularly working on, or interested in learning more about, and go straight to them, if you'd like. Then come back and read other chapters later, if you wish.

But to risk saying it once more: we think every chapter will help. And for the more linear-minded (and many of us are), reading straight through is a great way to go at this book.

* * * * *

Throughout the book, we will end each chapter with short tips. If you want a quick look back at the chapter, or some tips boiled down to a few lines—and possibly a new thought sprinkled in as well—go to those sections at the end of each chapter. We decided to have a little fun with it as well and show that writing is always a creative endeavor. Each and every tip will start with the letter from that chapter. (Yep, the Xs and Zs took a little more thought!) We'll cop to this point: some of the tips might overlap a bit, since we both put our own thoughts in this area. We see some overlap, but these are tips we personally like. So think of it as the more, the better!

*****

The companion to this book is *Mastering the ABCs of Excellent Self-Editing: Framing Your Colorful Masterpiece to Keep Readers Engaged*. If you look at the very words of that book's title, you'll see why we've split this project—which ultimately aims for one thing, to help you become a writer, or better writer—into two books. We'll say much more in the second book, but there is writing and then there is *self-editing*. (And we'll say more about this also, but the latter is not to be confused with hiring an editor to professionally edit your wonderful words.) Your writing produces an incredible story, fiction or nonfiction. But then you need to edit it, polish it, re-edit a bit more, probably, then probably polish a bit more. The second book will help with those steps. (If you doubt you need to self-edit your work before an editor has at it, we'll prove the need for that over in the second book.)

*****

In the end, nothing meaningful from your creative mind gets on anyone's reading stand or nightstand unless you the writer write it. So it starts with writing. And that's what this first book is about.

We do hope you find this little project helpful, insightful, and effective in improving your writing techniques. One of our chief goals is that it inspires you to become a writer, or to keep writing, or to write with a higher level of skill, whichever best fits your goals. So let's get started and create your vivid and colorful stories!

Contents

ONE

Get Them Reading, Keep Them Reading: Some Basics 15
Chapter 1 A: Action Words 17
Chapter 2 B: Bathe the Main Character in Peril 25
Chapter 3 C: Commas. 31
Chapter 4 D: Dialogue 45

TWO

Now for Some Real Flow 53
Chapter 5 E: Edit Only After Each Flow of Writing... 55
Chapter 6 F: Flavor of Writing. 63
Chapter 7 G: Grammar Is Secondary (and Yet Still
           Important) 69
Chapter 8 H: Head-Hopping Should Be Avoided..... 79
Chapter 9 I: Include Character Flaws 85
Chapter 10 J: Just Be Yourself. 93

THREE

Characters, Plot, Readability, and the Writer's Purpose 99
Chapter 11 K: Keep Plots Identifiable. 101
Chapter 12 L: Live in the Moment 109
Chapter 13 M: Make Your Main Character Likeable ..115
Chapter 14 N: Number of Characters. 119
Chapter 15 O: Overwhelm (Don't Do It to Your
           Readers) 127
Chapter 16 P: Point of View...................... 133
Chapter 17 Q: Question Why (Yet Answer with
           a Positive) 141
Chapter 18 R: Reality of Characters 147

FOUR
The Most Important Rule of Writing? Here It Is 153
Chapter 19   S: Show, Don't Tell 155

FIVE
Write for You? Yes. Write for Your Readers? Also Yes. 163
Chapter 20   T: Tense 165
Chapter 21   U: Unnecessary Words 173
Chapter 22   V: Vary Your Lengths: Sentences,
             Paragraphs, Chapters 187
Chapter 23   W: Ways of Writing 195
Chapter 24   X: X-ing Out Favorite Texts 203
Chapter 25   Y: Yield to the Flow 211
Chapter 26   Z: Zeal for Writing 219

Appendix A   Adjective Order in Lists (from
             Chapter 3) 225
Appendix B   Tense, Type, and Mood (from
             Chapter 20) 227
Appendix C   Words and Phrases to Avoid, or Limit,
             in Your Writing (Usually Unnecessary Words)
             (From Chapter 21) 233
Appendix D   Tips on How to Set Writing Goals
             (From Chapter 23) 239
Appendix E   Wonderful Writing Resources 243
Endnotes   245
About the Authors 247

ONE

Get Them Reading, Keep Them Reading: Some Basics

Chapter 1

Action Words

*"If my doctor told me I had only six minutes to live,
I wouldn't brood. I'd type a little faster."*
ISAAC ASIMOV

All verbs, as every English teacher we had in school drilled into us, are action words. That is true. But not all verbs are created equal.

Think of verbs as the engine of strong writing. No compelling story is told without action, and thus without verbs. From one of my (Bob's) favorite books, *The Day Christ Died*, by Jim Bishop, I pulled just one paragraph. It's not a pretty picture in the mind's eye—this is when Jesus is under arrest by Roman guards shortly before going to Pilate—but notice the action words.

Someone in the group had a more amusing idea. He got a cloth and blindfolded Jesus. The guards danced around him, cuffing his face and simpering: "Act the prophet, please. Who is it that struck you?"[1]

The first two sentences are setup for the scene. (The verbs are usual ones to get the paragraph moving: *had, got, blindfolded*.) But look at the next sentence: it teems with writing that captures the mind: *danced, cuffing, simpering*. What if Bishop had chosen, say, the verbs *moved, hitting, and asking*? (Quick exercise: replace Bishop's three verbs with the latter three. Done that way, the sentence then isn't even one-tenth as impactful.)

As this simple paragraph illustrates, all verbs are far from equal. Spend some time with your action words, and it will help drive your writing. But let's explore more.

Not only are verbs quite different, the terminology can be confusing. Ever hear the terms "strong verb" and "weak verb"? Even those tags can be confusing, and not everyone means the same thing when they use these terms. Let's keep digging. From English class, you were likely taught about strong and weak verbs from a structural perspective.

Weak verb is a term meaning the root of the verb doesn't change when you go from present tense to past tense to its participle form. Typically, all that happens is an -ed or -t ending is added. Here are a few examples (present – past – participle forms):

Walk – walked – walked
Look – looked – looked
Sleep – slept – slept

Strong verb, on the other hand, is a terminology meaning the root of the verb does undergo a transformation when its root is changed to its present, past, or participle forms. A few examples:

Run – ran – run
Bring – brought – brought
Swim – swam – swum

One takeaway here is the writer needs to understand that different verbs have different forms when their tenses change. After all, you want your writing to have strong grammar. Believe us, even readers who say they don't judge a book by its grammar do judge a book by its grammar. They may not realize this is what they are doing, but if your sentences "read funny," as some might say, their interest in your work will wane quickly. Only a few loose uses and you may well lose them.

So how can you tell which classification the verb is in? Unfortunately, you just have to learn them. There is no particular rhyme or reason. It just is, as they say. Therefore, if you don't know, then look it up. That's the best advice.

For writers, these terms mean something else entirely. When one says "use a strong verb," they are likely meaning to use a more appropriate verb, or one that conveys what you are really meaning, or one that brings forth the strongest action. Here are a few tips that, hopefully, you'll find helpful.

Adverbs

First, even if you have a strong feel for what an adverb is, let's define it. (You can find a more complete definition at Merriam-Webster.com.) The heart of an adverb is a word that modifies (expands on, explains further) a verb, adjective, another adverb, a preposition, a phrase, a clause, or even a sentence. But let's stay focused on verbs and modifying verbs here.

If you've used an adverb, see if you can think of a verb that conveys what you mean without the adverb. For example:

Harriet closed the door angrily.

Probably not a sentence one would normally write, but let's make the point more vividly here. So you can probably quickly think of a verb that coveys this meaning without having to use an adverb at all. Here's a somewhat obvious one:

Harriet slammed the door.

The verbs closed and slammed would both be considered weak verbs, by definition, but clearly *slammed* is a verb that conveys a door being *closed* in an aggressive manner and most typically in anger. This would, then, be considered a better verb to use. Some might say a stronger verb (and you could make that argument easily), not because of the structural definition that we just gave, but because *slammed* conveys the action you are meaning much better than does *closed*.

Another way to look at this is whether you must mentally ask yourself, as a reader, the *how* or *why* behind the word used. How did they close the door? Did they gently close the door, slam the door, or just close it in a normal fashion? *Why* did they close the door: to prevent someone from hearing them, because they were mad or angry, or it was just a normal everyday thing to do? If your verb doesn't convey this, then think of a more appropriate verb to use that conveys what you're really intending.

You may sometimes read to never use adverbs, but don't get caught up in this trap. I (Randy) did in the beginning. Here's a tip: when you read a blog from someone talking about writing and they use the word *never*, substitute *never overuse* in that spot instead. All forms of speech are needed to have strong prose and dialogue. However, as a writer, you need to master when to use each one. Granted, adverbs are to be used sparingly since there is typically a better or more appropriate verb you can use to convey the action (making use of the adverb unnecessary). So, the better advice, I think, is to use the verb that best conveys what you want the reader to take away from your writing. And make it a sentence in which the reader can get in the moment with you and not have to *think about* what you are saying, but be *with you* in what you are saying. You want your reader inside your story, seeing and feeling everything you are writing. You don't want them above the story, seeing it from a distance and having to analyze sentence structure to understand what you are trying to say.

Here is an example where an adverb is needed to convey what you really want to tell a reader:

Amanda sat quite still, daring not to breathe as the footsteps came closer, their sound hauntingly familiar.

Now one can get rid of the word hauntingly and change the sentence structure to avoid it. Yet most would find the sentence below doesn't convey the same tone and feel:

Amanda sat quite still, daring not to breathe as the footsteps came closer, their sound haunting her memory.

So, to reiterate this simple but key point, but said in a different way: *be purposeful in how you use adverbs.* Are you using the adverb to convey something (a tone, a scene, a feeling) that you can't do with a verb alone? If you can find a more powerful verb that conveys the same, then use it. If not, use the adverb to get your reader immersed in your story. Use them sparingly, though. A good adverb can enhance; too many can detract.

Passive Voice

I'm sure, like we both did, you also heard from an English teacher to always use active voice and never passive voice. Despite the bad rap, there is nothing wrong with passive voice, but again, it should be used purposefully and sparingly. Typically, passive voice does not get your reader immersed in your story. Active voice does. An example:

Greg had written the story for Ruth to enjoy.

Not a bad sentence as sentences go, right? But there is no real action here. Therefore, the following sentence would typically be better:

Greg wrote the story for Ruth to enjoy.

Or, if you can get it in present tense, it is even more impactful:

Greg writes the story in the hope that Ruth will enjoy it.

It just has a fresher feel to it and is more engaging, isn't it?

But judging passive voice by sentence alone does not quite do it justice. There are definitely times to use passive voice. Once again, though, with a purpose. Remember to always be purposeful in whatever you do as a writer.

Here's a trick to the "dreaded, to be avoided" passive voice: it can be extremely effective in setting a scene. One example:

John's travels had been torturous and taxing. He had received not a wink of sleep for three days. None of his travel companions understood the stress he had been under before he left. They were so absorbed in their own problems they had no time to consider his.

So this sets up a scene. Now, if the whole scene would be written in this manner, it would become quite boring. But this can set up an action scene. The passive voice fills the reader with knowledge, and then an active voice pulls them into the story with that knowledge. Again: be purposeful.

A * A * A * A * A * A * A

More Tips and Information (Summing Up, and Perhaps a Bit More)

From Randy, the Author

- **A**lways use verbs that best paint the action you are trying to convey.
- **A**dverbs paint a mood or setting. Use them sparingly so they have maximum impact.
- **A**ttempt to use active voice when possible.
- **A**void passive voice, when possible, except for scene-setting or to show that a large amount of time has passed between scenes.

From Bob, the Editor

- **A**re you using verbs as the engine of your writing? Drive your writing forward with impactful verbs.
- **A**sk yourself: does this verb feel a little flat? Try another, or another. You might find another action word works better. Actively compare.

- **A**void doing this all day long, however, with every verb. That's not possible, and you need to get on with your writing. But do go after the ones you know can be improved. Usually, you'll find them. (Or maybe a good editor can help in certain cases. Do the work on the front end, however, and your product will be better for it.)

Chapter 2

Bathe the Main Character in Peril

"Get it down. Take chances. It may be bad, but it's the only way you can do anything really good."
WILLIAM FAULKNER

By putting your main character in peril, you allow your readers to sympathize with their plight and begin to bond with him or her. So you want strong action words, but then you also want your main character involved in action. In many cases, the quicker the better. You want your reader to be *in* the story with your main character, joining them, emotionally, as quickly as possible. Putting your character in some type of peril helps achieve that. And once you have your reader bonded, you most likely will have them for the entire book.

Now, when we say peril, we don't necessarily mean you have to create the next Indiana Jones book/series. Peril can be physical, mental, emotional, or spiritual. (As a simple example, think Jean Valjean in *Les Miserables*. The key moment comes early when he steals the bishop's silverware and silver plates. Not the most egregious crime in history, but it is the fulcrum around which the entire story builds.) So, your peril needs to be something your readers can identify with so they can root for your character, be their biggest champion, fight with them, cry with them, and rejoice with them when they are victorious.

You can't make life easy for your main character. If everything is wonderful, how will your readers identify? After all, the lives of your readers are likely not pinwheels and roses either. They know life can be difficult. They want a character with whom they can identify. But let's balance this: they don't want constant gloom and doom either. They want to escape into a world which will take them into the lows but not leave them there. Heights and victories are also needed so they can feel joy and happiness with your character. But the main character *must* have hardship.

Your main character needs to be a real person—not fake. This is not to say that your main character doesn't have character flaws. Actually, your main character *needs* to have character flaws. (Think Jean Valjean.) They need to evolve over the course of your manuscript. Perhaps they are a fake person, but they need to become a real person by the end. First, get your readers to identify with your character. Then they will be with that character as they break out of their fake shell into a person the reader can rejoice with when things do work out in the end. As we said, peril can be a lot of things, so let your imagination soar. The main thing is that you get your reader into the story as quickly as possible.

A further point: peril is not a once-and-done thing. You do need to bring your main character or characters up for air occasionally. If it is all too depressing, you will lose your reader. But don't think everything has to be happy. Even in a concentration camp, one can experience moments of joy and hope. Make your characters real. That is what your readers want. It doesn't matter if their circumstance is in a concentration camp, on a moon of Saturn, in an intergalactic war, or in the middle of a love triangle—your characters need to develop and grow. Being placed in physical, emotional, or spiritual peril will allow them to do that and take your readers along with them.

Can villains be a main character? Absolutely. Again, though, you must make them identifiable with your readers. They may not like what the villain is doing, but if they can understand the motive or flaw that makes them the way they are, you'll have your readers alongside them. For example, I (Randy) had a character in my novel *Iron in the Scepter,* named Janet, who used her children for her own gain. Sound horrible? Yes it does. But that's not how I started. I introduced her as an ambitious woman who, over time, lets pride cloud her judgment. The reader is taken along with her. The reader wants her to make the right decision. She almost does, but then doesn't. The reader is not turned off by her decisions but is certainly saddened about them. It's like having a friend who you want to make good judgment calls but who often doesn't. You don't abandon them; you still root for them to make the right decision next time. Think Anakin of the Star Wars saga. You know how he will turn out, but despite that you root for him with all your energy. You want him to not make that decision you already know he is going to make! This doesn't turn the reader off but glues them even more strongly to the character.

So everything is on the table. It's up to your imagination in how and who you develop and incorporate in your storyline. Just know you are also bringing readers with you. They don't know you or your character yet. Introduce them, create a bond, and then plunge them into deep lows and great highs, and they will ride the roller coaster with you until the very end.

* * * * *

Let's look at this from another angle and show how it's true in several ways.

First, think of any story that compels you to keep reading, or watching, or listening. There is always conflict (peril). Go ahead; choose something that has grabbed you through the years. Maybe you're a Harry Potter nut, as my (Bob) kids and about 99.2 percent of their generation were. Think of *The Hobbit* and *Lord of the Rings* trilogies. Bilbo Baggins is a regular old hobbit living an amazingly boring and never-dangerous life when twelve small but mighty dwarves and one wizard compel him to an adventure in which he is never quite out of danger. In *Lord of the Rings,* his nephew Frodo Baggins is in constant pursuit in the land of Mordor and his attempt to destroy the ring while every peril imaginable comes after him: orcs, trolls, Bolg and his warriors—even a *thing* called a Gollum.

Think of any movie that inspires you; there is always peril, there is always something to overcome.

Now take the Bible. David is held up as one of the central characters of all sixty-six books, a shepherd boy who sang songs and took care of sheep. Sounds dreadful, right? Before his life was over, however, David was a warrior, a victor, a young man in flight from deadly danger, an older man in flight from deadly danger (his own son), an adulterer whose poor decisions led to the death of many, and a man competing for the affection of various women, other warriors, and at times all of Israel. His life would read like an amazing piece of fiction were it not that the Bible declares his story to be true.

Last, look at *your* life. Seriously. What parts stand out? The times when you grow the most, when you most feel like you are *living*, are when you overcome something difficult, some conflict, some peril. Here's just a small-scale look at this (though certainly more momentous things happen in life). I (Bob) recall taking a leisurely evening stroll with a group, while at a writers/editors conference, in the Blue Ridge mountains; the goal was a summit called Rattlesnake Peak. (I know, right? No, we didn't run across any.) There was no danger, and we felt a good bit of exhilaration in reaching the summit just before evening, viewing a beautiful sunset upon our arrival. It was in coming down that the real adventure began. It got dark—pitch-dark—causing us to lose our way and worry about the bear warnings that had been posted. And all sorts of engaging conversation (we'll leave it at that) and searching ensued. Thankfully, everything worked out in the end. Those are the times in which every fiber of your being is invested, when you feel alive and engaged.

* * * * *

As we said, the perils can be many, but do create an overarching danger, or conflict, your main character or characters must overcome. And just when the reader feels the main character has made it, the bottom must fall out again before they overcome in the finale. This can be done in various ways. Let your imagination be your guide. Your readers will love you for it.

B * B * B * B * B * B * B

More Tips and Information

From the Author

- **B**y all means, put your main character in peril as soon as possible.
- **B**e sure to endear your reader to your main character as early as possible.
- **B**rand your main character with a redeeming quality in some way, even if they are the villain.
- **B**efore the end of your story, make it seem the main character has overcome their crises—and then plunge them into another before final resolve.

From the Editor

- **B**ecause a manuscript with conflict and peril keeps your readers (and yes, even a good editor) engaged, be sure to add peril. With a good book, even as I edit, I can't wait to see where it is going.
- **B**attling conflict is the main stuff of life. Not all conflict is good for humans, but it certainly is for readers.

Chapter 3

Commas

"I'm writing a first draft and reminding myself that I'm simply shoveling sand into a box so that later I can build castles."
SHANNON HALE

Certain writers, as you can imagine, sometimes overuse commas, and others underuse them. Let's get this out of the way: there are a plethora of rules around how to use commas. But here is the first rule: don't be intimidated by that! You, us, *all* writers... learn as we go. One more quick note about this chapter: it's going to be a tad longer, because using commas well is important and distinguishes you as one who is thoughtful about her or his writing, or not.

The most important rule with commas is to ensure that the proper meaning of what you are trying to convey is indeed shown. Perhaps you've heard this very basic but humorous example, which has been put on T-shirts worn by nerdy people around the world:

Let's eat Grandma.

Let's eat, Grandma.

Commas save lives.

Funny, but it does drive home the point. You want your reader to not be confused about what you are saying to them or what thoughts, ideas, or messages you want them to understand. Again, many readers may not understand the rules of commas, but they will know when they are not used effectively, so this is an area we as authors need to understand.

As a final preface to this chapter: not only will this one be a tad longer but also a bit technical. Take your time working through it if you need. (See our Preface instructions at the beginning of this book.) Good comma use, however, is critical. Nothing sets off a writer who still has much to learn versus one who is getting more advanced at the craft more than . . . understanding the use of commas.

So let's dive in.

Some of the rules can be confusing. One reason for this is how the rules are communicated. One example is that some have said a comma should be placed before any conjunction: *and, but, for, nor, or, so, yet.* This "rule," however, is not always true, so it's not a very good "rule." A more correct way of saying this is that independent clauses separated by these conjunctions will have a comma before the conjunction. An independent clause is very simple: a portion of a sentence which, if it was pulled out of that sentence, could stand as a full sentence (essentially, noun plus verb) by itself. See these examples:

I love you, but I can't stand your habits.
I love you but not your habits.

The first sentence is composed of two independent clauses: "I love you" and "I can't stand your habits." Both clauses could stand as sentences on their own. The second clause is tied to the first by a condition.

This is not the case in the second sentence. The phrase "not your habits" is not a standalone phrase. In its own right it cannot stand as a sentence. Therefore, a comma is not required.

Here are a few others. These can be phrased more technically, but we've shown them in these ways so they can be more easily understood. (We hope those of you who stand on technicality can forgive.)

Clauses and Phrases

Clauses placed at the beginning of a sentence, often called introductory clauses, generally need a comma. To illustrate:

While on the phone, Amy filed her fingernails.
Amy filed her fingernails while on the phone.

As we can see, if the phrase is at the end of the sentence, no comma is needed. But if you place it at the beginning of the sentence, it needs a comma. The introductory clause is not, in its own right, a sentence. Therefore, a comma is needed.

These clauses will typically start with words such as *after, although, as, if, since, when, while*. A test, if you will, is that if you put the clause at the end of the sentence and it makes sense, then it needs to be separated from the rest of the sentence if you choose to place it at the beginning instead.

Let's move on. There are sometimes phrases at the end of sentences that will need to be separated from the rest of the sentence. Typically, these are phrases adding contrast. They are not independent clauses, so they can't stand on their own as a sentence, and they would not make sense if placed in the beginning of the sentence. Here are a few examples:

I said I was simple, not ignorant.

You are coming to the dinner, aren't you?

Sometimes, single words need to be offset with a comma from the rest of the sentence. Often this will be one of the following words: *however, well, yes, yet*. But the biggest key: read for sense. There is a natural pause after the first word in the two examples we provide just below. You might argue that you don't need the comma, but in reality, if you think of listening to someone speak the sentence aloud, you do. (This, by the way, is another very good rule of writing: read your sentences aloud. We'll say more about this later.)

Well, thanks for the advice.

Yes, I plan to do that tomorrow.

Then there are phases within the middle of the sentence that may need to be separated by commas. These typically give additional information that, while helpful to the reader, is not essential for making the sentence a meaningful sentence. Another basic way to look at this: if you pull out the middle clause, the sentence is still fine. More than fine. The middle clause says something—and it can even be very important!—but if it were pulled out, the sentence would still fully stand. A few examples:

Mary loved this book, which she had read a hundred times, but allowed Jamie to have it.

John looked at Susan, who he thought beautiful, and displayed a bright smile with a wink.

Your work is usually exceptional. In this case, however, your typical quality is lacking.

As usual, there are exceptions. One exception is a phrase that begins with the word *that*. These phrases are typically considered essential whether they follow a noun or a verb:

The cow that you milked is now in the pasture.

The cow being milked that kicked over the pail will need to be restrained.

There are also essential phrases that will not need commas even though the sentence could still be a proper sentence if the phrase is taken out. (Don't you just love the English language?!) A way to know whether a phrase is an essential one—one that doesn't need commas versus a non-essential phrase needing commas—is if you can identify the subject without the phrase. Take these two:

The lady who is carrying a red purse said she likes Bill a lot.

Betty, who is carrying a red purse, said she likes Bill a lot.

We know this can be subtle, but you can see the reason, right? In the first sentence you need the phrase to identify which lady you are referring to. In the second sentence, you already know who she is because you've called her Betty. Therefore, in the second sentence the phrase is helpful, but non-essential to identify who you're referring to. (There are all sorts of little ways to remember these things until they're ingrained in your head, so use what works for you. One way we've heard is: in the second sentence, think of the independent clause as not needed to make the sentence proper, thus it's somewhat weak, thus it needs lifted up, or supported by, if you will, commas. In the first sentence, the phrase is critical to know who in the world it is who's really into Bill!)

Next, there are phrases that can be placed almost anywhere in the sentence and will need to be offset with commas. A few:

Lisa waved good-bye, crying incessantly.

Crying incessantly, Lisa waved good-bye.

Lisa, crying incessantly, waved good-bye.

However, when more than two subjects are in the sentence, you must tie the phrase to one of the subjects for clarity. Therefore, the phrase cannot be separated from its subject. For example:

Lisa waved good-bye to Larry who was crying incessantly.

Lisa, crying incessantly, waved good-bye to Larry.

In the first sentence, it's clear Larry is the one crying. In the second, it's clear Lisa is the one crying.

Moving on: commas are also needed for lists. This can be a list of words, phrases, or clauses if there are three or more elements in the list.

I like apples, pears, bananas, and mangos.

If I see you there, hear that you stopped by, hear that you called, or even find out you sent someone on your behalf, you will be in big trouble.

Now, I don't know if you were taught like me (Randy) in school that the comma before the conjunction is optional, but my editor always has me put a comma before the conjunction. There is a risk of creating confusion if you don't. Therefore, put the comma after each element of the list when there are three or more elements.

Now an aside from the editor (Bob): the last comma that Randy referred to is called the serial or Oxford comma. (The first relates to dealing with a series of items, not anything more nefarious.) Simply, it just makes things clearer. *Chicago Manual of Style,* the bible of excellent writing rules, tells you to use it. (It also seems a bit more academic which, even if you are writing something intentionally goofy or lowbrow, makes you look just a bit smarter. Which is a real aside, but there you go.)

I was once given this silly example. While intentionally silly, it still makes the point. The first sentence carries that proper comma. The second is for those who want to be a rebel and not use the serial comma. I think you'll see the point, and while this is somewhat goofy, other non-uses of the serial comma can, basically, leave a lack of clarity.

> *Joan said her life's inspiration were her parents, the Pope, and Mary the mother of Jesus.*
>
> *Joan said her life's inspiration were her parents, the Pope and Mary the mother of Jesus.*

Whoa. Without the serial comma, Joan had one amazing set of parents, no?

Adjectives

What about when more than one adjective is next to each other? Do you put a comma between them? Even if they are in a list? First, ask yourself if the order of the adjectives can be interchanged. Then ask yourself if the word *and* can be placed between them still allowing the sentence to make sense. If the order cannot be interchanged, then no comma is inserted; if the order can be interchanged, a comma is needed. Two examples:

Amy's son is such a happy, content, and articulate young man.

Amy's son has two large, muscular, Indian, close friends he works out with regularly.

In the first sentence the adjectives *happy* and *content* can be interchanged and the sentence still makes sense; therefore, a comma is inserted. The adjectives *content* and *articulate* can also be interchanged and the sentence make sense; therefore, a comma is inserted. However, the adjectives *articulate* and *young* cannot be interchanged and still make sense, so no comma is wanted in that spot. To complete this sentence, a comma is placed between *happy* and *content*, while the *and* comes before *articulate* rather than before young.

In the second sentence, all the adjectives can be interchanged except for *two* and *large*. Therefore, commas are placed between each of them except between *two* and *large*. If you read it with an *and* between *two* and *large*, or if you interchange their order, it just doesn't sound right. Therefore, there is no comma between *two* and *large*.

When two or three adjectives are in the list, the order is somewhat dependent upon what you are trying to emphasize. Yet when the list gets longer, the decision of order becomes more complicated. While such a long list of adjectives would be rare, experts in the English language have come up with a natural order in which adjectives would be listed. This has been placed in Appendix A in the back of this book, but the order, in general, is expected to be quantity, opinion, size, condition, shape, age, color, pattern, origin, material, type, and purpose.[2,3]

Dates and Places

Next, commas are used with places and dates:

Cary said he was raised in Oakland, California, in the 1990s.

Cary was born November 25, 1998, in Oakland, California.

For Effect

Sometimes you'll need to add a comma when it is not technically necessary. This could be done to create a pause in the flow of the sentence because perhaps it is too long, or done to add effect or emphasis that helps propel the thought being presented. An example:

"But I saw it was you who rescued me."
"But I saw, it was you who rescued me."

In the first sentence, the person is acknowledging who rescued them. In the second sentence, the person is having a self-revelation, of sorts, of who rescued them.

Sometimes you may not put a comma where, technically, it should go. This helps propel the reader along rather than make the reader mentally pause when that is not a place that truly needs a mental break. One example:

"Yes, sir. I know the diamond was stolen."
"Yes sir. I know the diamond was stolen."

Although subtle, the second sentence gets the reader to the important fact faster. There is no mental pause, as is in the first sentence. While the first sentence is technically correct, you may opt to not have the comma there. Sometimes you will want it there.

Watch and listen for the flow of your story, which is one of the most important things. In the first case, the speaker maybe has a lump in his throat and realizes he needs to confess to an understanding. So he pauses. If that's what you intend to convey, comma needed! In the second, the speaker is maybe a bit brash, unafraid of admitting this knowledge, bold before his inquisitor, and just wants to blurt his answer as quickly as he can. So he does not pause. No comma!

Let's move toward a bit of sum-up on this chapter.

As you can see, it's sometimes logical where commas go, but not always. Hopefully the information provided proves helpful. Yet we can't stress enough that you really need a good editor who can help in this regard. Editors are essential. The reason I (Randy) say this is that, first of all, it's true. They can help identify many of the places a comma should go, and they are trained to know why commas are needed in certain places. Yet they're also attuned to the flow of your story and will know when not to follow the rules. And the flow of the story for the reader is more important than the technical rules.

But there's still one more area we need to cover in this chapter. Because it is so closely related, we'll sneak it in this chapter instead of a subsection in chapter S: *Show, Don't Tell*.

Semicolons

To close, let's talk about **semicolons**. In school, maybe you were taught that semicolons can be used in place of a conjunction. Rather than the conjunction combining the two sentences, the semicolon does that. However, our advice is to use them with caution and not a great deal of abundance. The two sentences, or independent clauses, need to be tightly associated so that the reader is not stumped in trying to figure out why you used a semicolon rather than a comma and conjunction—or just a plain period and two sentences! Therefore, be judicious. Also, think about flow. A semicolon adds a mental slowdown; it is a sort of period, a mental stop. (Read that sentence again to see the effect.) If a conjunction interferes with the flow just a bit, but you don't want the reader to have a mental stop, then maybe a semicolon is a good alternative. But remember: too many semicolons will be distracting and wind up destroying the flow rather than enhancing it.

An important bottom line: your writing is not about how grammatically correct it is, although good grammar is indeed important! Good writing, in the end, is about how it flows and pulls your reader through the story, unencumbered and unconfused. Never forget: your reader is paramount. All you do is for your reader so he or she will enjoy and get lost in your story.

* * * * *

Come Alongside Your Reader

Can't help but ask. Have you ever heard any public speakers do the following? This is not at all meant as a bashing of faith here, or preachers, but have you ever listened to a sermon or some kind of message and the speaker kept saying things like, "You need to . . . . " Or, "You're not being successful in that area . . . " Or, any other of a number of "You're not . . ." phrases?

The opposite of coming alongside your reader is talking at your reader, or worse: *down* to your reader. Immediately the listener—or reader, if it's in your writing—feels like they're not doing enough, not good enough, not able to . . . and on and on.

Which of these is more attractive?

You're disappointed in your daily Bible reading? How much do you want to read your Bible? How much do you tell yourself, "I must read my Bible." Did you take time to put a reading plan together (as we talked about in chapter 1)? Did you set your time and stick to it? If you didn't do these things, you have to question yourself.

You're disappointed in your daily Bible reading? Welcome to the human race! I remember I struggled with this for years—and, in fact, still do. With the help of God and friends who showed me better habits, it's improved a good deal. But I still have those days where it feels like absolute drudgery to start my reading. I've improved, but I have more to learn. As I wrote in chapter 2, I often turn to friends for ideas or shared reading times together.

The answer is not even close, right? Both paragraphs talk about self-disappointment, and both talk about better habits and disciplines. But that's about where the similarity ends. Readers who feel the author is alongside them can't wait to keep reading.

Readers who feel the author is talking down to them may stick with it for a while . . . but then, fairly soon, the book gets set aside with the reader's thought of possibly returning to it, but he or she rarely does.

Conversational Writing

Conversations are what people relate to. In this shortest of our sidebars, we give yet one more C: write conversationally.

We hope the entire book conveys this, but wanted to say it in this one space. Make your reader enjoy feeling you are alongside them. Imagine you are both comfortable on two couches, you are relating a story, and they are just soaking it in. You want them to not want to close that book for the night; only tired eyes force them to do so. There is academic writing, but that is not what you're doing here. (You might, at some point. But most writing is not on that level.)

We like to refer to the classics a good bit. Read John Grisham, or J.K. Rowling's Harry Potter books, or just any great author. You're inside a story, not laboring through it. That's what we're shooting for with 99.9 percent of our writing.

C * C * C * C * C * C * C

Tips and Information

From the Author

- Commas are essential to good writing; therefore, learn the basic rules surrounding them.
- Can you break a rule? Yes, but have a good reason for doing so, and know why you broke it.
- Commas are extremely useful to aid in the flow of your writing.

- Creative flow should not be restricted; therefore, worry more about commas during the self-editing phase of your writing. Do attend to good comma use, but first . . . write.

From the Editor

- Comma efficiency is imperative. While this repeats Randy's first rule above, spend some time learning basic use of commas. You don't have to be perfect, but you should find improvement in a short amount of time. Few things are as frustrating for a reader as a writer who has no mastery of the basic comma.

- Coming alongside your reader is important, especially if you are writing non-fiction. Don't talk down to your reader. Join them where they are with your common struggles.

- Conversational writing is a goal to strive for. Your readers should feel as though they are snuggled up on a couch with a good friend when reading your work.

Chapter 4

D
Dialogue

"Writing a novel is like driving a car at night. You can only see as far as your headlights, but you can make the whole trip that way."
E. L. DOCTOROW

Designing dialogue can be difficult, can't it? But wait: it's just people talking. What's so hard about that?

Well, there is dialogue, and then there is strong, effective dialogue.

First, let's get the mechanics out of the way. What the person says is provided within quotes so the reader can know what is actually being said by someone. What a person says is typically a paragraph unto itself. The attribution of the quote is separated from the quote itself by a comma. (We didn't cover this comma use in the previous chapter since we're doing so here.) In addition, the attribution is typically the noun followed by the verb. For example, which of these two sentences reads more naturally?

"I just loved that book," said Jane.

"I just loved that book," Jane said.

Hopefully you chose the second sentence. That's the way most would write it and read it—unless you are Master Yoda, perhaps.

There. Done. Is that all there is to this? Yes and no, but mostly no. While that is the general mechanics, strong dialogue has an artistic element as well. But this art has—well, not rules—but things to think about as you create dialogue. For instance, you could write the following:

"I just loved that book," Jane said.

"I did too," Art said.

"What was your favorite part?" Jane asked.

"Oh, the ending, for sure," Art said.

Not very riveting, is it? Consider this revision:

"I just loved that book," Jane said.

"I did, too," Art said, breaking into the conversation.

Jane looked at him, somewhat annoyed. "Really? What was your favorite part?" She had never seen Art read anything before.

"Oh, the ending, for sure."

Now, we wouldn't say this revision is the most riveting thing you have ever read either, but you get more out of the second conversation than the first. The first is just a bunch of quotes strung together. Now imagine your entire book is written like that. Did your eyes go wide? We hope so. That type of book would be ghastly, wouldn't it? The revision, however, has actually told a story, and you did that through dialogue with some prose mixed in. We actually see tension between Jane and Art—not something you can pick up in the original set of sentences. While not gripping, it is certainly more interesting, yes?

Did you also notice that not every quote in the revised example had attribution? Yet it was clear who said the words. That's important. You want to use attribution when necessary to ensure the reader does not get confused as to who is speaking. But you don't want to use attribution too often, as this becomes stilted writing and can make the dialogue drag and interfere with flow.

When you have more than two characters in a dialogue, attribution becomes more important. It becomes easier for a reader to become lost as to who is saying what unless attributions are used. Yet, even here, you don't have to use attributions with each and every line. Clear inference as to who is speaking can be used to help with flow. And even if there are only two characters talking, if the conversation is long, you need to add attributions every so often to keep it clear in the reader's mind who is saying what.

I (Randy) once heard a famous author say they had written an entire novel without using attributions. Now I suppose that is entirely possible, but believe me, doing so is much harder than it sounds! I attempted the feat, thinking my novel would read much better without all those *he said, she said* attributions. And since each piece of dialogue becomes its own paragraph, the reader would know a different person said the words because they were contained in different and separate paragraphs.

While, technically, that is true, doing so doesn't prevent the reader from getting lost. I found that out when I got the manuscript back from my editor who, to my chagrin, added attributions! He kept saying things like, "I didn't understand who said this here. I assumed it was person so-and-so." Originally, I pushed back, saying it was obvious because it was another paragraph. Thankfully, he was patient with me and helped me see that readers don't necessarily look at writing techniques to get their cues. After all, many readers likely don't even know why dialogue from each person is in a separate paragraph. They go by the writing itself to draw their cues. And, after all, as we've said, *your writing is all about your reader.* If they get lost in your dialogue, they will eventually cast your book aside. That is not what you want! I eventually concluded that if my editor got lost in the dialogue, so would my readers. I'm glad I listened.

In addition, and what may help you, is to consider your book as an audiobook. The reader is only listening and not looking at a written page to know if the dialogue is in a separate paragraph or not. Only your words are giving cues, to the listener in this case, as to which character is speaking. If they get lost, then they can't follow the storyline and will, at some point, lose interest.

Actually, that is a strong writing tip overall as well. Read your manuscript out loud to yourself. Or have your computer read it aloud to you. (Many word processing programs have that feature now.) While the computer won't be able to put in the emotional aspect of your story, it will help you find several types of flaws in your writing: spelling errors (because the word will be pronounced wrong); syntax errors (the sentence will just "sound funny"); dialogue attribution (you may get lost as to who is saying what); repeating words or phrases (the repetitive nature of these will sound monotonous). There are likely other flaws as well that may become obvious, but you get the point. This is a good habit to develop. We'll say more about this topic later in this book.

Let's move on. The attribution doesn't always have to go at the end of your dialogue. This can help break up some of the monotony when you must give many attributions. Sometimes, put it in the middle:

"I don't know why I came. You're such a bore," Jill said.

"I don't know why I came," Jill said. "You're such a bore."

Both are legitimate sentences. But something about the second just rings as a little more interesting, right? Remember, it's all about flow for the reader. If you break up where the attribution is provided, it can help with dialogue flow.

In addition, the attribution doesn't have to be at the end of a sentence as in the example above. It can occur within a sentence itself, but always after a completed phrase:

"Well," Julian said, "your example didn't make any sense to me."

"Well, your example," Julian said, "didn't make any sense to me."

Do you see the difference? The second example just won't work. The attribution is within the middle of Julian's thought. In the first sentence, the attribution is at the end of a phrase that is complete, albeit a very short one. This is not the case in the second sentence. The sheer number of words is not always the determining factor. Whether a complete phrase has been used or not, is.

Regarding what verb to use in the attribution, most writing teachers will tell you: 98 percent of the time, use the word *said*.

And they are right. Why, you ask? The chief reason is this attribution verb becomes almost invisible. Readers come to expect it and read over it almost as if it isn't there—if the dialogue is good, that is. If the dialogue is poorly written, it will stand out. If the dialogue is written well, it won't. In truth, if you are looking to change the attribution verb to make your dialogue sound less monotonous, you should focus on the other aspects of dialogue and not the attribution.

So what about the other 2 percent? There can be times you may want to use another verb. Examples would be if the person is asking a question, making an emphatic statement, or adding tonal quality. Here are a few examples:

"And what texture would you choose for the dress?" Sue asked.

As the tree began to fall, Paul shouted, "Timber!"

As the boys crept down the stairs, Greg looked back at Bill. "Stop pushing," he whispered.

All of these may be used some of the time, but certainly not all the time. You are trying to pull the reader into your story. You are not adding variety for variety's sake but adding what fits into what is taking place in your story. Variety does not change bad dialogue into good dialogue. Variety enhances good dialogue. It can never save it.

One final point. Attributions should be physically possible. For example, one can *say, ask, shout,* and *whisper.* Yet one *cannot* laugh, snort, or wheeze words. You would not say:

"I can't believe you said that to him," laughed Gregory.

But you could say:

"I can't believe you said that to him," Gregory said with a laugh.

Live in the real world. Your readers will appreciate it. This may not seem like a big thing, but readers notice. And some of your reviews may reflect that. Don't give readers ammunition. Trust me, they'll find bullets on their own!

So, in summary, live the conversation you are writing. If your own writing pulls you in, it will likely pull in your reader as well. Put in appropriate attributions when needed. Make the conversation flow like a real conversation. When it is long, put in attributions periodically, but don't break the conversational flow. Use a variety of attributions as needed, but sparingly, and use attributions that are physically possible. These simple but effective techniques will take your dialogue far. Always remember, you want your reader *in* the conversation with your characters, not *reading* the conversation of your characters.

D * D * D * D * D * D

Tips and Information

From the Author

- **D**ialogue between characters requires attributions so readers know who is speaking, but too many attributions become distracting.
- **D**ialogue is like prose in that it should flow smoothly for your readers.

- **D**o mix up attributions so some come during the dialogue and some at the end.

From the Editor

- **D**ialogue characterized as strong dialogue does at least two things: it adds depth to characters, and it provides a variance in the reading pattern for the reader.
- **D**ismiss dialogue that only says the most mundane things. Skip it entirely. Show the scene instead. (Much more to come on this in chapter *S: Show, Don't Tell*.) As an example:

    "Hand me the bowl," she said angrily.
    "Okay," he reluctantly replied.

    ... That construction is a big loser to this one:

    She glared at him incessantly until he finally placed the bowl in her hands.

- **D**raw your reader in with strong dialogue. There is nothing quite like conversation and the human exchange of important ideas, conflicts, and joy.

TWO

Now for Some Real Flow ...

Chapter 5

Edit Only After Each Flow of Writing

"The most valuable of all talents is that of never using two words when one will do."
THOMAS JEFFERSON

Every seasoned writer and editor will tell you: don't edit as you go. Now, that is good advice, but like anything else, don't become obsessed with following it as an absolute. This doesn't mean that if you happen to misspell a word or need to add a word or phrase to what you have already typed to not do so. (Do so. And fix the spelling since it's staring you in the face right now, so you won't somehow miss it later.) What this so-called rule is implying, though, is that you should not interrupt your creative flow by editing as you type. There may be times you are on a roll and typing furiously to get your thoughts into

the manuscript; then it is certainly all right to not correct spelling as you go or to not think too critically (at this writing moment) about how you said something. By all means, get those thoughts down.
You can make it pretty later. In fact, you *will* make it pretty later.

What we want to emphasize, though, is to never, never, *never* use editing as an excuse for not pushing forward with your writing. Editing should not become a procrastination habit. Don't let yourself develop the habit of feeling you are creating your novel or book when you are editing. If you have not completed the first draft of your novel or book, then no, you are not being creative; *you are procrastinating.* Editing becomes part of the creative process only when you have your first draft completed.

Now, again, at the same time, don't take what we've just said too literally. Don't let rules stifle you. Then they become antihelpful things and destroy your better judgment. And we're not saying to never go back and read anything you have already written until you have completed your first draft. We will often go back and read a chapter to refresh where we're at in our writing, especially if picking up where we left off the day before.

A bit more from Randy: It could be that a thought came to me that I forgot to add within something I have already written. Now, as I am reading back through that chapter, I may correct a spelling mistake, an attribution error, or do a little wordsmithing. But the overarching point is: at this time, that is not my main goal. I am just getting my mind back in the game, so to speak, so I can start where I left off. The major editing will come once the story has been told.

There could be a valid and justifiable reason you want, or need, to edit a chapter already written. It could be that you need a better version of that chapter for your thoughts to become clear as to how to move the plot, character development, or overall narrative (in a nonfiction book) forward. Then, by all means, do so. Yet we would still say that you don't have to make this chapter pristine at that point. That will come later. Get it to the point that propels your thoughts forward, something like removing a single large rock that is impeding a stream's flow.

There are two types of editing. One is correcting spelling, syntax (we'll define that word shortly), attribution, and word choice errors, or any type of grammatical errors. The other is content editing. The latter deals with the issues at a bigger-picture level: is the flow correct, are subplots explained well, are all questions you have placed in your readers' minds answered and addressed? Now, if you're writing a trilogy or series, then all subplots and questions don't have to be answered in your first book, but you should have a good idea as to when those subplots and questions will get resolved. While this will be addressed after your first draft, you should keep this in mind as you write so you can have a plan for how you are going to resolve these things. After all, this could decrease the amount of editing on the back end if you have addressed subplots and questions you have placed in your readers' minds in a purposeful manner as you write. Consider keeping a list of the subplots and questions so you can be sure you haven't forgotten to resolve something by the time you reach the end of your writing.

It's also important to say this: make these rules and suggestions work for you. Don't let them rule you as to how you write or make you feel, "Oh, I can't do that." This is *your* masterpiece. Do what you need to do. Just don't let any of this stifle your creativity or flow. Strong flow in writing is critical. For instance, you may know you used too many words to describe a scene, or you could have described a person's clothes better, or made a section of dialogue crisper. It's all right. It will get cleaned up when you get to intentional self-editing.

Also, develop your own technique as to what works best for you. For example, maybe your juices are really flowing, and your fingers are flying due to all your creative synapses firing. You come to a scene where you really need to do a lot of description of where the characters are, or what they are wearing, or how creepy something looks, yet you have all these action ideas in your head that you need to get down before they're gone. That's okay. Get the action down and then come back and add in the other details and descriptions. As you are zooming along, you can just write a note—right there in the manuscript, maybe with a colorful highlight behind it, to remind you to come back and do strong cleaning up in that area. Your note might say "describe clothes" or "describe complicated detonation sequence," and you'll come back to that detailed description later. That way you can get the important points down that are in your brain *now*. It's not that the description is not important, but what's important at that moment is what is in your brain.

No one says writing must be sequential. Perhaps you are struggling with a certain aspect of your story, but your mind is vividly clear that once your hero gets out of the current mess you've placed him or her in, you know exactly what should happen. Go ahead: put those scenes down and come back later to the scene you're struggling with. As you go through what is clear in your head, that may give you the clarity needed for the scene you are struggling with. You can always tie everything together in the end.

The point is to do what works for you. Get the creative flow down when you are in the zone. Don't create barriers to your creative side coming forward and flowing. Editing is an important aspect of your final creation (our second book in this series is going to cover it), but not an important aspect of your first draft of *writing*. First drafts are messy; they just are. Expect them to be. You can tidy somewhat as you go, but deep cleaning comes at the end.

There are other resources you may find useful on this point. Another book I (Randy) have used is *Self-Editing for Fiction Writers: How to Edit Yourself into Print* by Renni Browne and Dave King. Much of their information we have also covered, but it could be helpful to read the same topics from a different perspective. It can also give you a more rounded view and more ideas of how to be a better writer.

* * * * *

Explaining Content and Copy Editing

Editors intuitively understand the difference between content and copy editing. As a writer, you don't have to be perfect at this. But to get the sense is important. *Copy editing* is all the nuts and bolts, as Randy said: spelling, grammar, style, best syntax, things of this nature. (Syntax is a big word that confuses people, and it has nothing to do with having to pay the government for bad things you have done; that's called a *fine*.) Syntax deals with the proper arrangement of words to make a sentence clear, flow well, and read logically for the reader.

Content editing, as we referred to above, is the bigger picture. Think of content editing as achieving great planning on where items are going to go in a newly built addition to your house. Copy editing is the small stuff like mounting that big-screen TV in the right way and in the right place on the wall, cornering that bookshelf well, things of that nature.

For geeks and those who just want to know, there is an even higher level of editing (higher up the development process, we mean) that is called *developmental* editing. This is planning the entire house. This is the blueprint for the house. This must be done well also, of course. But many authors have a good sense for the overall direction of where the book is going, so they don't need this help. Some do need this help. Lots of famous "authors" do. They have good stuff to share from years of experience, but they have no idea how to put it all together. A good editor can help at this level as well. (There's still one more level up the chain, and that's the "author" who couldn't, as is sometimes said, write their way out of a wet paper bag. They can't write anything with even a modicum of skill. They've built airplanes or driven race cars or been in war combat numerous times, and thus have amazing life skills, but they just can't write. Who helps them? That person is called a *ghostwriter*.)

Let's bring it all together. Have the *content* stuff well developed in your mind and . . . write at a strong-flowing content level. Only worry about the copy editing later, coming back to it, after the flow of a section, or even long section, is in.

One more reality? You're going to need a good editor to work on your manuscript after you're all done. But if you have written well, followed this pattern well, you're going to have a far better product. (We'll say much more about working with an editor in the second book in this series.)

E * E * E * E * E

Tips and Information

From the Author

- Editing, or at least the main effort of editing, should come only after your first draft is complete.
- Engaging in major edits before the first draft is finished is to procrastinate your writing efforts.
- Eliminate the idea that you have to write sequentially. You can tie pieces of your novel together during the editing process.
- Ensure you get your ideas down before you forget them—then come back later and tie them all together appropriately.

From the Editor

- Even a good editor who is a writer is going to need a good editor to edit her or his book. (Everyone needs a good editor!) What's the point? Write for strong flow and pace, because you're going to come back and edit anyway, and someone else will be (or should be) helping final edits after you're done.
- Engrain this in your mind as one countering point to this entire chapter: don't think your writing is so gold-

en you can do it in one swoop, barely look back, and it's magically ready to go straight to your publisher's printer! You *do* need to go back over your writing, and there will be rounds of editing. The main point of this chapter is to not get so bogged down in that task that you're not . . . actually writing.

Chapter 6

Flavor of Writing

"Never write anything that does not give you great pleasure. Emotion is easily transferred from the writer to the reader."
JOSEPH JOUBERT

Formatting your story requires you to decide on its flavor. We're not talking about your genre or style of writing, but about how you want the reader to perceive your story. By that we mean to decide if you will write in first, second, or third person. This is something you need to decide before you begin because you don't want to change this critical aspect in the middle of your writing, and you don't want to mix these as you write.

Now, you may think up creative ways to combine different reader perceptions in one novel or book, but doing so takes much planning and should be done with purpose. This can, conceivably, be effectively achieved, but it needs to be well thought through so your readers won't become confused with what you are doing. Therefore, be sure you have mastered these perspectives before embarking on trying to combine them.

The most common way of writing is in third person. Most books you find will likely be written in this way. And it's true that first person has become much more popular as well. And we have to say, we haven't seen much writing in second person, period. Someone likely has, but neither of us has seen a novel written in that way.

Let's go back through. Writing in third person is the most common perspective because it is the most diverse of the three and, we think, is the way most people normally think and write. When one decides to write most kinds of documents, third person is what typically comes out without the writer having to consciously think about things. It's just more natural to say, "Michael did this," or "Michael thought that." When you write in third person, you will use pronouns like *he, she, it, they,* and their derivatives. After all, that is why they are called third-person pronouns.

Yet even if you are writing in third person, there are three different views from which you can write: limited, objective, and omniscient. We will go into these when we get to chapter *P: Point of View.*

As we said, writing in first person has also become popular. This does take more of a conscious effort because everything is from *your* perspective: the "I" perspective. It's telling a story from the main character's experience. Your goal is to have your reader identify—intensely so—with the main character and place themselves in the shoes of that main character. When you write in first person, you will use pronouns like *I, me, we, us,* and their derivatives.

First person can make the reader more intimately involved in your story because, as the reader, they can more easily place themselves in the main character's shoes. Again, though, this is only true if done effectively. Just the choice of first person does not automatically get your reader personally involved in your story. Conversely, even if the reader doesn't like the character, first person allows a closeness to the thoughts of your main character. No matter which voice you use, your goal is to get your reader personally involved and engrossed in your story.

Second person is likely the most difficult, though not impossible. As the writer, you are actually addressing the reader and placing them in your story whether the reader wants to be there or not! You, as the writer, will be using the pronouns *you* and *your* throughout. If the reader identifies with your character, this can make a very tight bond between the reader and the story. Conversely, if the reader doesn't like your character, this choice could turn them off entirely and they may think "I would never do such a thing" or "I would never think that."

Another way second person can be used effectively is if the overarching narrator of your story uses it to pull the reader into the story by asking them to imagine a certain scenario, and then you, the character in the story, use first or third person to tell the story itself. So there are ways to use second person, but it is definitely the most challenging of the three perspectives.

The bottom line is to use what you feel works best for your story and what you feel will bring your story to life for the reader. Just using any particular perspective, however, will not do that by itself. What you choose must be executed well, with intention, purpose, and determination to skillfully pull your reader in without them knowing they have moved from reading your book to actually being in your book. If they have come to the end of your book or novel and are emotionally sad because there are no more words to read, you have definitely been successful.

F*F*F*F*F*F*F

Tips and Information

From the Author

- Fix in your mind, before you begin, if you will write in first, second, or third person.
- Flexibility is the best attraction for writing in third person and likely the reason it is the most used of the three.
- Format your writing so you stick to the choice of first, second, or third person throughout your novel or nonfiction book.
- Flow broken by backstory—perhaps telling a dream, or a character telling a story to another character—is a place where one could switch, say, from third person to first person, but for that section only.

From the Editor

- First person works well in a memoir or autobiographical work, but that is usually not a new writer's first work. (If someone with a great deal of life experience writes a memoir as their first book, this can work.)

- Fewer cases of first-person writing work well. But here's one in which it can: the right kind of non-fiction book.
- Framing your writing in third person, as Randy listed above, is not only the most common, it is also likely the easiest to write in. It's probably the best place for a newer writer to start.

Chapter 7

Grammar Is Secondary (and Yet Still Important)

"Close the door. Write with no one looking over your shoulder. Don't try to figure out what other people want to hear from you; figure out what you have to say. It's the one and only thing you have to offer."
BARBARA KINGSOLVER

Grammar? Huh? Everyone knows it's important, but no one wants to think much about it. Grammar is a bit like vegetables on your plate. You know you need them, they're actually essential, but they sure ain't the highlight of that steak dinner you're looking at. (And no, don't use *ain't* in your writing—unless in a well-placed portion of dialogue. Or like here, used merely for effect.)

So let's take a step back. By the name of this chapter, we are in no way implying that grammar is not important. It is not only important, it is essential.

First: let's be clear on what grammar is. It's a smallish word that leaves people saying, "What? What *is* it?" Is it a school for young kids? Is it something only bespectacled English teachers or primpy British people care about? Is it just the last name of some well-known actor? (Okay, yes, he spells it Grammer.) Do we need to know what good grammar is?

Yes, yes we do. But here's the good part: Much of it is common sense. Much of it can be answered by whether the sentence reads properly and not "funny," as we'll mention again just below.

So let's clear the decks first. What's a good definition of grammar? You can go to lots of dictionaries, but we chose to go to *Chicago Manual of Style* (known the world over as CMS) which, by the way, is among our recommendations as an indispensable writing tool. (Side note: CMS is long and thick, but don't be overwhelmed by it. You will read it only in small chunks. It is not a writing tool you will sit and read from start to finish. When you pick up CMS, you'll know what we mean.)

In short, grammar is the strong, common-sense use of words that carries the reader along in a crisp fashion, not haltingly. CMS defines grammar this way:

"Grammar is the rules governing how words are put together in sentences. These rules, which native speakers of a language *learn largely by osmosis,* govern most constructions in a given language. The small minority of constructions outside these rules fall mostly into the category of idiom and usage"[4] [emphasis ours, not CMS].

So there is no question grammar is important. Let's be clear on that. And we are addressing strong grammar throughout this book.

But we now reach the main point of this chapter: reader flow is *more* important. Grammar will be in your face your entire life, so most of the rest of this chapter will step outside the normal uses and address the second part of that CMS use: "constructions outside these rules."

But first one more reiteration of the first point, that grammar is necessary: even readers who say they know nothing about grammar and that they don't think it's important to like a book will more than likely get turned off if they find themselves reading poor grammar. Why? Because it will "read funny." The reader may not be able to articulate the reason behind why she or he feels the text is "off," but the reader will know what sounds proper and what does not. After all, we are accustomed to hearing good grammar, and most know poor grammar when they hear—and read—it.

So word choice should always be grammatically correct. The only time when it is sometimes acceptable to not be correct is in dialogue. If one of your characters has a manner of speaking with poor word choice, or contractions, or in a certain manner, then it would be acceptable to avoid good grammar.

Your character should be whoever she or he is, and let their natural speech flow from there. Mark Twain was a master at this in his novels.

Still, here are some key things to consider.

If all your characters speak with broken English or in a certain manner, it would still probably not be acceptable to have your entire book have dialogue in broken English. It would likely serve you better, and your readers to accept your book better, if you set the backdrop of how everyone speaks in this geographic area where your characters live and interact. Then go with acceptable, strong grammar. Your readers are smart enough to pick up the atmosphere you are creating for them.

If one of your characters has a speech impediment or a way of talking differently from the other characters, perhaps consider giving an example here and there at crucial parts of your book, but use regular grammar elsewhere. This keeps the essence of your character alive without having your readers wade through all the stuttering or broken English to figure out and understand what is being said.

If you have a character from another country who, for example, uses a v-sound for a w-sound, it would likely be better to either use a few examples and then switch back to normal spelling, or, perhaps even better, explain this trait and then use normal spelling throughout. You can always draw attention to this characteristic by the reaction from other characters to this character's attribute. As an example, I (Randy) had a character like this in my book *Mercy of the Iron Scepter*. I said the following to cover this trait: *She had a thick Slavic accent. Her 'w's had a thick 'v' sound, which Kalem found intriguing.* This allowed me to then continue with normal spellings without having to continually change each 'w' into a 'v' to show how she would pronounce certain words. Remember, your readers are smarter than you may think. They don't need to be reminded at every turn of something you want them to understand. For the most part, they will get it and likely appreciate you not reminding them on every page.

There is a choice that can be made, though. Your character's dialogue may be very unique, or perhaps the character doesn't appear throughout the book. Then you may want to use the strange characteristic with every dialogue use for consistency.

We have talked about what can be called reader flow. For the most part, when a reader must wade through all these irregularities, it slows them down. Sometimes that's good, but sometimes it is not. If your readers are made to constantly wade through broken English spelled as broken English sounds, this slows their flow, and they may even forget what the main thought of the plot is because they are so focused on trying to understand what this one character is saying. Hence, the reasons for the suggestions above.

While we have said that grammatically correct word choice should almost always be chosen, there is latitude for correct punctuation. Some of this was mentioned in chapter *C: Commas*. Punctuation rules can be your friend or enemy. It is important to know the rules, but also important to know when to break them. And it is vital to know when you have broken them. As we have stated a few times already, everything should be done with purpose: you should know your why behind the reason a rule was broken.

Sometimes you want the reader flow to slow significantly because you are creating a dramatic scene or feeling. In this case, you may make sentences out of single words, or short phrases, that are not sentences. This is perfectly acceptable because the moment is calling for it. Here is an example.

Susan turned with anger in her voice. "Stop it, Jeremy! Just. Stop. I can't take it anymore." She put her hands over her eyes and sobbed.

Consider the individual words made into sentences: this would not be considered grammatically correct, but you are using poetic license with punctuation to create a strong effect for the reader. Adding the periods between the words causes the reader to pause, and this adds emphasis to demonstrate how upset Susan is. And this is how people, especially angry people, talk, so your reader will not think this a strange use of punctuation.

Ellipses can be used for a similar effect.

Susan turned with anger in her voice. "Stop it, Jeremy! Just ... stop. I can't take it anymore." She put her hands over her eyes and sobbed.

Also, notice that since this is no longer separate sentences but the same sentence with a pause between key words, the first letter of stop is not capitalized.

However, if you use these techniques all the time, the reader will do one of two things: think your character is just melodramatic—and therefore the technique will not have the emphasis you intended—or just skip over it mentally because they've seen it several times already. You've broken the rules. It should be for a reason. It should be an exception and not the norm.

Sometimes you might add a comma or punctuation when it is not needed for the intended effect that your reader can take a breath or mental pause even though the sentence structure doesn't demand its use. This could be because you have a long sentence, or maybe you want your reader to pause and consider what they've just read. And it can be merely for effect.

Paul solved the puzzle no one else could, and with ease.

Another way to do this would be to add an em dash (the longest of the dashes) instead of the comma:

Paul solved the puzzle no one else could—and with ease.

We can see there are actually a number of ways to create the feel and drama you wish your reader to experience.

Another rule breaker, and one we talked about in *C: Commas,* is to not use a punctuation which would typically be included based on the rules of punctuation. The reason is to not break the flow for the reader so they can get to the main point. Repeating our earlier examples:

"Yes, sir. I'll get right on it."

. . . could instead be:

"Yes sir. I'll get right on it."

In the first sentence, your mind pauses after the word yes. In the second it does not, and your mind quickly flies onward. The second creates the effect of answering in a more military-like fashion: "Yes sir." No pausing, no doubt. You say it, *I'll do it.* That is the effect you're looking to get across.

Now, please understand that we're not saying you can break any and all rules. For example, if you run two sentences together so the reader doesn't stop, that is very likely not a good thing—it's just the dreaded run-on sentence. (This is a sentence that clearly breaks the rules of grammar and punctuation by flowing on to multiple small sentences. A run-on sentence could even be short. An example: *Paul solved the puzzle with ease Susan was befuddled how he did this.* That's actually two short sentences and certainly, because it's so bad, will make your reader fall out of her chair, or close your book!)

Remember this ultimate point: your work is all about the reader. Stamp this in your writing mind:

If it confuses the reader, do not do it.

If it helps the reader, it is likely that poetic license can trump a basic rule. But first you need to know the rules! This book and others recommended in this book are good sources that can help with a strong general knowledge of grammar. Again, you should break a rule for a purpose—an intended purpose—to achieve a desired effect either for your reader or in your reader. Your reader is queen (or king, as the case may be)!

G * G * G * G * G * G * G

Tips and Information

From the Author

- Grammatically correct prose should always be implemented.
- Going away from proper grammar, however, for your dialogue to create a specific effect for a character's personality or upbringing is fine.
- Giving a few irregularities in your writing can make a story interesting; a story full of irregularities can quickly become tedious for readers.
- Graciously keep your readers in mind for any deviation from the norm: balance quirkiness against tediousness.

From the Editor

- **G**rasp a strong, general knowledge of grammar. Start there.

- **G**o with the most basic rule for all your writing that does not fall into the exception category: use common sense for strong grammatical writing. We recommend *Chicago Manual of Style* to check where you're not sure.

- **G**iven any sticky parts you're not sure about, *after* you have written for flow (see our earlier chapters), ask a friend with some editing background skills to look at your sentence, paragraph, or section you are wondering about. Ask them if you are displaying strong, questionable, or poor grammar.

Chapter 8

Head-Hopping Should Be Avoided

*"You write to communicate to the hearts and minds
of others what's burning inside you, and we edit
to let the fire show through the smoke."*
ARTHUR PLOTNIK

Head-hopping is a term that refers to when a writer allows the reader to hop from one person to another within the story they are reading to know the thoughts of each. Is this something that should be avoided or allowed? Different people have different views. So we'll give some rationale for both and then see if there is any common ground.

For some, this is frowned upon as it's considered unrealistic to the world in which we live. For example, if you are in a conversation with another person, you can't know what that individual is thinking. You can only infer what you *think* they may be thinking based upon visual cues. So just because you as the writer know what's going on in the minds of all the characters in your story, this doesn't mean the reader would, or should, know.

From Randy, a novel writer's perspective:

While you can change whose thoughts the reader is knowing, they should not be able to know all at once. The change should be made when a scene is completed. In most of my novels, I only have the reader travel through the story knowing the thoughts of the main character and maybe one additional key character, but never those two at once. For example, in one scene from my book *Mercy of the Iron Scepter*, several people are waiting for the main character, Kalem, to arrive. This scene was presented through the eyes of another key character, Angela. Then when Kalem arrived, I switched the reader to see things through his eyes. The reader no longer knew the thoughts of Angela which they had just been able to know. This was done several times in this novel, but again, never at the same time. The reason I did this was because I had several subplots for the reader to understand.

* * * * *

Previously in this book, we talked about the omniscient view as an acceptable way of imparting information to the reader. Yet this omniscient view is typically from the all-knowing narrator who doesn't get into the minds of the characters themselves as it imparts knowledge to the reader. Even if the all-knowing narrator were to go into the minds of the characters to do this, it would still be better to only have the reader know the thoughts of one character at a time, and, as stated above, to only change when a scene changes.

Often, to denote there is a change in perspective, the writer will put a series of asterisks, centered, between the paragraphs of each scene to denote the change, like this: * * * * *. (Hey, we used that convention just two paragraphs above!) As an aside, the other time to use this technique is if a substantial period of time has occurred between two paragraphs. These are good visual cues to the reader so they don't become confused when things switch or when time is skipped.

Okay, you may have a rebuttal that there are authors who do not abide by this non-head-hopping rule. That could be the case. I (Randy) read that head-hopping is often done in romance novels so the reader can get wrapped up in the emotions of two characters simultaneously. That actually makes sense, doesn't it? But again, that is done with a marked purpose, not a casual one. In this particular case, the reader would likely not get confused because it is only between two characters. Yes, if you go beyond two, definitely think a good deal on this (among other things, perhaps).

We've hit on only the key component here. Will the reader get confused? If readers are allowed an omniscient view of everyone's thoughts, can they keep what every character knows straight in their minds? The characters themselves certainly do not have this capability: one of an omniscient view. If readers are receiving only the thoughts of one character at a time, they are better able to keep that aspect with clarity. Plus, we think it helps readers to engage better as they try to figure things out along with the characters rather than knowing things the characters do not.

Also, keep in mind that just because you use the omniscient view for your story, you still don't have to reveal everything at once. You should reveal things in a piecemeal fashion to make them more interesting for the reader even though you, the writer, already know where things are going. You don't have to tell it all—at least until the right time is revealed for the reader.

Once again, we come to the same critical point we have said before. It's all about the reader. What will give the reader the most engrossing experience without having them endure a jarring mental break in concentration, leaving them wondering where they are in the story? Do they have to stop and think: *What does this character know or not know?* Once more, to repeat: do what is best for your reader.

Typically, as we've said, the best way to provide an omniscient view for your reader is for the narrator to provide that view. Essentially, the narrator is an ambiguous force imparting knowledge to your reader. Yet some would argue this is "telling" and not "showing" (we'll cover the difference in a later chapter). As they say: all things are permissible, but not all things are best.

You are the creator, designer, and architect of your story, but everything you do is for your readers. Whatever pulls them into your story and keeps them captive is best. Don't keep them at a one-thousand-foot view, and don't make them labor to think about which character knows what. Give them everything they need to become immersed in your story.

H * H * H * H * H * H * H

Tips and Information

From the Author

- **H**ead-hopping should only be done between scenes or chapters.

- **H**old to this point carefully: make it obvious to your readers where the point of view has changed to avoid confusing them.

- **H**elp your readers better enjoy your story by revealing only what they need to know at the time. That keeps them in the story along with your characters.

- **H**owever you inform your readers through your story, your readers should not know more than your characters.

From the Editor

- **H**opefully, your readers are reading along because they are engrossed, not because they are trying to figure things out. For the most part, a one-character view makes this a reality.

- **H**ard bottom line here: don't make your readers have to work needlessly to figure out where things are going. One of your jobs is to keep things simple enough that they want to stay engaged.

- Help your readers along if there is a change in point of view or significant passage of time by giving them a visual breaker (such as * * * * *) between paragraphs. (When your book is designed, the design and layout expert might have other ideas or even appropriate symbols, matching the book's feel, for this breaker.)

Chapter 9

Include Character Flaws

*"The true alchemists do not change lead into gold;
they change the world into words."*
WILLIAM H. GASS

Interest is destroyed by perfection. Perfection can be a goal or an ending, but not a beginning. Your readers can't identify with perfection. After all, who can? We live in an amazingly flawed world. Who's perfect? No one you or we know. Even heroes have flaws.

Flaws are what build the connection between your readers and your main character. Even if your protagonist appears perfect, he or she needs to possess a flaw, or flaws, that readers discover, even if other characters do not know about them. You want this to happen so your readers can identify with your character, suffer beside your protagonist, root for him or her in the process of overcoming, and cheer when your hero does overcome. Typically, your main character has a flaw, works to overcome it, and, just when he or she almost does, the bottom falls out, only for your protagonist to rise to the occasion and finally become victorious. Remember one of our points under 'C': come alongside your reader? This is another form of making that happen—and doing so through your storytelling.

Now when we say *flaw*, we're not speaking about a physical flaw or defect (necessarily). Your character certainly could have one or more of those, but that is more like giving your character an identifying characteristic. For example, they may have a limp, a bad case of acne, or their hair may never seem to stay combed. But these physical flaws could affect them emotionally in how they interact with others, explain the reason for their shyness, or why they try to become wallpaper in a crowded room. Those are the types of flaws that reach a reader's soul. These types of emotional flaws are harder to overcome, and when your character does triumph, your readers are more likely to celebrate alongside your hero.

Think of Superman. You're not introduced to him as Superman, but as Clark Kent. He is a mild-mannered reporter. One perceived as weak, always late, never on the scene at the right time—a good guy, but never the *right* guy. He's the underdog. So when you find out he's Superman, you're like: *Yeah!* Now he's the man in charge, the one everyone looks up to, wants to be like, and who gets the girl! Your readers can identify with this because that is a secret longing for almost everyone. They likely often feel like the underdog—at least sometimes they do. So make your character vulnerable, likeable, and identifiable, someone others can identify with. Let's face it. Not every character can be Superman. But every character with a flaw can overcome that flaw in some form or fashion to become a better version of themselves.

"But my main character is a villain," you may be saying. That makes it harder, but not impossible. After all, no one likes the bad guy. But you can still make him or her identifiable. This can be achieved by having the character have some redeeming trait or reason they became the bad guy. Make your readers like them before they become, or before you show, their inner darkness. A perfect example is Anakin Skywalker. Before you met Anakin, you met Darth Vader, and you knew how bad and evil he was. Yet Anakin started out likeable. You knew he was going to turn to the dark side, but you still hoped he wouldn't. And you were still sad that he did—even while knowing full well he would! Anakin was unquestionably likeable, so likely your view of Darth Vader changed as well. You still saw him as the villain he was, but you now had a better appreciation of why he became evil. You still hate what he did, but perhaps you do not hate him as a person anymore. Knowing his background changed your perception of this infamous character.

From Randy: In the first book of one of my series (*Mercy of the Iron Scepter* of the Stele Prophecy Pentalogy series), the mother of the main character is introduced late in the story and you, as the reader, hate her immediately. You are likely turned off by her from the moment of her introduction. Yet the fifth book of the series (*Iron in the Scepter*) becomes her story (going into her backstory). By the end of this book, you are left feeling sorry for her rather than hating her. You still didn't like what she did or had become, but you better understood her, her motives, and how she came to be who she was. She was a person blinded by pride. She became more identifiable because you know people with a similar problem. While you never come to the point of necessarily liking her, you come to a better understanding of her and her motives.

Again, your goal is to get your readers intimately involved and engrossed in your story. As we've said, this can be because the reader identifies and loves your character, or he or she just can't believe what the character is doing and tries to will them to better choices. Because you made this character full of pride and selfish, and yet identifiable, your readers will not abandon them even if they don't really like them.

*****

Italics: Do's and Don'ts, Goods and Bads

Included here is a very different I from the main topic of this chapter: the use of italics.

So what about the use of italics in writing, or placing a *special* emphasis on a word or words? (Did you detect a misuse of italics in the previous sentence? If you thought you did, you were correct.)

Here is, perhaps, a decent way to think of it: using italics might be like consuming a good hot fudge sundae. Now, you might enjoy one of those hip- and heart-busters, maybe, once a week or every couple of weeks. But if you had one following every meal of the day, you'd get pretty unhealthy pretty quickly. Not to mention, you'd get pretty sick of them.

Italics can have their place, just like an occasional ice cream splurge. I (Bob) have seen new authors who wish to italicize so much material that any real impact of the use of the convention is, by necessity, lost. (Picture a college student yellow-highlighting material in a text or on their laptop who just can't stop using that highlighter. After about two pages of it, nothing stands out anymore. The use itself becomes pointless.)

We have mentioned *Chicago Manual of Style (CMS)*. You can learn a great deal about correct use of italics from CMS. Entire books could be written on this subject, so we don't want to use up too much space here. But let us quote CMS to show a bottom line: "Good writers use italics only as an occasional adjunct to efficient sentence structure. Overused, italics quickly lose their force. Seldom should as much as a sentence be italicized for emphasis, and never a whole passage."[5]

There are so many nuances to good uses of italics that we encourage you to read and learn what you can, and you'll learn along the way. We are not saying you need a perfect grasp on this before you consider an italics use. You will keep learning as you go!

There are clearly times to use the convention to stress the key element in a sentence. The CMS section cited just above gives this example:

How do we learn to think in terms of *wholes*?[6]

According to the sentence, what's about to be discussed (wonky as it sounds) is *wholes* (versus fractions)—that idea, that concept. So it's right to lay some special emphasis on the word. This is the idea. You can look back through this book and see various uses of italics in our work. Guess what. Some writers would argue against some of those uses! Writing is rarely a perfect, locked-down, the-rules-never-change exercise. And yet you also want to write well, with proper emphasis, not over-emphasis. Again, who truly wants a hot fudge sundae fourteen times a week?

Again, there is much to learn with this topic, but we'll provide two final side notes: *CMS* will say the exact same things about capitalizing an entire word for emphasis (it's the same idea, but now looks EVEN MORE amateurish) or putting words in bold font **just to emphasize them**. (More can be learned about rare but proper times to use bold fonts.)

The following *are* proper uses to italicize, per nearly all accepted styles: titles of books, music CDs (albums), newspapers, and magazines (*Catcher in the Rye, White Album, Chicago Sun-Times, Newsweek*) and, believe it or not, names of ships (the *USS Enterprise*).

One other use: thought, or inner dialogue, by a character. (*That was a horrible day,* he thought. *It couldn't have been worse.*) You do this because to put quote marks around the words would imply having spoken them aloud. Instead, this is thought in the character's mind.

Final word: this is a convention to use, but sparingly!

I * I * I * I * I * I * I

Tips and Information

From the Author

- Indubitably, your main goal is to get your readers engrossed in your story from the start.

- In your writing, your main character doesn't have to be likeable—but needs to at least be considered redeemable.

- Include flaws of some kind in your character(s). This is an excellent way to endear them to your readers.

- Invariably, you want your readers to root for your main character or, if a villain, at least not willing to abandon him or her.

From the Editor

- Italics (I'll keep my tips on this chapter to italics, since Randy, above, has covered character flaws well): use them sparingly. Study good writing in many forms; you'll see proper uses, and you'll see they are needed (and wanted) only sparingly.
- In order to learn about style, read appropriate sections in *Chicago Manual of Style*, or other style books. You'll start to get the hang of things fairly quickly.
- If a use of italics stands out to you as probably or possibly unnecessary, it probably is. This is really important to get right, *don't you think*? (Yes, that was a totally lousy use of italics.)
- I saved one of my favorite personal rules for italics for this last tip: let the strength of your writing carry the day. Have confidence in it. If you have to italicize to make a sentence really pop, maybe the sentence isn't all that strong on its own.

Chapter 10

J
Just Be Yourself

"If you can tell stories, create characters, devise incidents, and have sincerity and passion, it doesn't matter how you write."
SOMERSET MAUGHAM

Joking from Somerset Maugham aside, you have a story to tell. There's something burning inside you that you really want to say. This chapter is going to deal almost entirely with your passion to tell your story. And only you can tell that story. In the way only you can tell it.

This leads to The Idea. (Your idea. For a great book.) But your idea must spring to life. I (Bob) had a coworker in publishing who once told me, "Dear, I've got a drawerful of book ideas. But I'd have to quit my job to write them." She felt her full-time job was keeping her from doing the hard work of the full-time job of writing. So something has to springboard your idea into existence. Someone must birth it. It will take commitment. And it will take time.

Now, you may have a full-time job, and you may feel just like my former coworker. Even though you can't write full time like King or Steel or Grisham, you can still write. It will come slower, perhaps, but you can still make it even if the final product comes much more slowly than you wish.

If the story is fully your idea, the only person who can tell it is you.

Initially, the idea can be euphoric. *My gosh,* you think, *that's brilliant.* No one's written that, I'm sure. Until you discover that, yes, someone has already written your brainchild. (Still, that can be okay, because your perspective can be unique.) Initially, the idea can be energizing: *All I need to do,* you tell yourself, *is write a thousand words a day, for fifty days, and I'll have fifty-thousand words.* It holds until about, say, day three sets in. Initially, the idea can be euphoric. Until . . . you look at the costs you may have to incur, start thinking about marketing, the critical author marketing piece, and all the online worlds you want to dive into, and you start to get overwhelmed. Initially, euphoria fills you until . . . the doubts start to crash in.

But here's the important point: if you have a story to tell, and only you can tell it, a true writer's passion will push you to keep pecking at that keyboard. It's in there—inside of you. The words will keep coming out. Many a new author has expressed this sentiment: "Seeing that book to completion was like giving birth."

I (Bob) have been privileged to work with a long list of authors. Most are quite normal people who just have something to say, such as a number of women who have lived through horrific abuse, survived, and now help others survive their darkness.

I found it a privilege to help them tell their story. Or a man, now a friend, who has overcome mental illness and the darkness that drove him to the brink of suicide—but found God's grace instead. Or a World War II veteran who decided, at age 89, to write his war memoirs. Or maybe a man who watched his young, beloved wife die and persevered through that horror, only to have her speak to him, post-life, in a way that was so real, so convincing, he was certain it had to be her.

All just normal people with something to say.

So start writing. See where it goes. It's going to take many twists and turns, work and rework, anyway. Follow where they lead. Don't be afraid of all those starts and stops leading to unexpected left- and right-hand curves.

I (Bob) love the little ditty of a song by the Beatles, "Paperback Writer." Not one of their all-time greatest, perhaps, but a jaunty little tune. Look up the lyrics for fun. A man is determined to be a writer. He'd love to sell his book. He asks the publisher, "sir or madam," to "take a look."[7] That's essentially it. And that's really what it's about for anyone, isn't it? Pushing the story that you have to tell out there.

Lots of people want to be a writer. Anyone can be a writer. It doesn't mean you'll make money from the final product, or become famous. But you can write. So first determine what you want to say.

Don't forget: your writing is you. These are your words, driven by your passion, carefully crafted by your thoughts and ideas, and maybe even your ideals. You want readers to identify you with your writing style, your plot conceptions, and how you put your stories together. Don't try to be like anyone else or write like the style or voice of another. Even if your story is similar to that of another author, it will and should read differently.

We know there are some authors who look for whatever genre is currently the popular, hot topic and then write in that target area. While that is certainly a viable approach, we would caution about that choice for two reasons.

First, you need to understand and predict what will be the hot topic and genre when your book will come out, and not what it is when you first start to write. This takes some predictive ability as the market could be different than you expected. One must really understand their audience, the genre market trends and volatility, and what the consumer in a particular genre market wants and demands. Also, this type of writing typically means you must produce a book relatively quickly to accommodate the trends and demands. So, while not impossible, certainly, it does make it more challenging since knowing the wants and demands of your intended audience must become almost second nature to accommodate those expectations before they change too drastically. This adds an extra layer of stress that may not be suited for all authors. So, bottom line, know your audience, but more importantly, know yourself.

Second, it will likely be difficult to be new and fresh in your ideas for the book because your heart is not fully in the story. It will take a lot more effort and discipline to write in this manner. You will be writing not from passion for the story but from passion for what you think the readers want. So ask yourself if you really know the inner workings of your audience. If you do, that will be more than half the battle in producing a marketable product. Also, if you can become passionate about the same, all the better. What we're simply saying is that writing from someone else's passion is far from the easiest motivation.

What is likely easier, and more fun, as an author is to write from your own passion. That will make the thoughts and creativity flow far more naturally. While it's true you are the one writing from this inner passion, we think there are consumers for each and every author's passion. While the number of that audience can vary depending upon the genre you write in and your unique writing stye, there are likely many readers out there who will appreciate what you produce.

So be yourself. There is an audience waiting for you. Granted, some audiences are harder to find, but they are there. And once they find you, many will be devoted.

J * J * J * J * J * J * J

Tips and Information

From the Author and the Editor*

- Juxtapose your passion with your writing and the enthusiasm for your story will come through to your readers.

- Judging yourself against the standard of other writers is not healthy as you should not try to be like any other writer. Readers are intuitive and know if your writing is genuine and comes from your passion.

- Jealousy is demotivating, so be realistic with your expectations for being an author. Success comes with time.

- Jumping into wealth may not happen quickly, so you might as well hear it: don't expect to make money with your first book, and likely not with your first three to five books. (Or not much, anyway.) If this holds true, you're

> like most authors, so don't despair. In your first book or books, you're getting yourself out there. But you're also learning a craft. And you are winning the war of writing and having fun along the way.
> - **Just be yourself.** An audience is waiting for you. You have a story to tell. Work on telling it.

* This one is so critical, we decided to just meld things into one set of tips. In other words, we're very closely aligned on this one!

THREE

Characters, Plot, Readability, and the Writer's Purpose

Chapter 11

K

Keep Plots Identifiable

> *"You can make anything by writing."*
> C.S. LEWIS

Know that a story can have many plots, but there should be one overarching plot for the reader to grasp. This main thread throughout the story is somewhat like the lifeline for the reader. Maybe a better metaphor would be a trail of breadcrumbs for the reader to follow. This main plot involves the main character, the one character you get your reader to care about or be most interested in. As stated previously, you want your reader to latch onto your protagonist and come along for the ride with him or her.

The reader should be along for both the emotional ride as well as the physical one. You get them to feel what the character feels: experience the highs and the lows, cry and laugh with the character, and even get mad when something or someone harms them in some way—or even become angry at the characters themselves because they are making bad decisions. You want your reader to care for, and be invested in, your protagonist. The overarching plot propels the reader through your story because they care about the character you have created.

Now that doesn't mean your reader won't care about other characters in your story as well. That's where subplots come in. These make your story more interesting, add depth, and increase the complexity and interest. After all, life is like that, isn't it? Your life is not one-dimensional. (Granted, sometimes we wish it were, as that would make things a lot easier to manage, but it wouldn't be as interesting, would it?) Your story needs the same: interest and complexity. It makes the reader feel your story is real, plausible, and worth experiencing and investing their time with the characters you have created. Now when we say *real* and *plausible*, we don't mean what you have created is necessarily real and plausible in real life. Yet if you've created your world well, whatever that world is, your reader will have bought into all the caveats you have devised for this place, and what the characters go through will be considered plausible and reasonable.

While you may not be a science fiction fan, I'm sure you have friends who are. When they get excited about a book they have read and they're telling you about the story with great enthusiasm, they'll feel compelled to tell you all the small details about this world they've become immersed in. They want you to understand what they are saying is real and plausible in the world in which they have entered. (As fantastical as they are, when you think about it, this is exactly what the entire *Star Wars* universe, and pantheon of creative series deriving from it, do: they immerse people.) That's what you want to create for your readers: for them to feel at home in the world and within the story you have created.

Also, realize that all the plots and subplots you create must resolve. All do not need to be tidied up with a nice bow on top; after all, life doesn't work like that. Yet your reader has invested herself in your story and wants to come out on the other side satisfied. You don't have to make the reader happy at the end, but she or he needs to feel the time investment has been worthwhile. So keep track of all the plots and subplots you create in your storyline, and be sure they get resolved in some form or fashion in the end. If you're writing a trilogy or some type of series, that allows you more time to resolve certain plots and subplots.

Don't forget, though, that each book needs to supply the reader a "good investment" feeling at its end. That means that certain plots or subplots need to have some kind of resolution by the end of the book for the reader to gain the full experience. There are many ways to accomplish this. But we think they all boil down to a few variations that fall into two main categories.

Resolution. (1) The plot resolves with the character or characters never having to worry about that particular issue again. If you are writing a series of some kind, this is an issue that should not resurface in a later book. Something related could surface, but not the same issue. For example, the villain is killed or dies, and the threat is completely eliminated. (2) The plot resolves but with the idea that it may not have completely resolved or that the issue, while fine for now, could possibly resurface. For example, the villain is killed or dies, eliminating the immediate threat, but that villain has a son who may later seek vengeance. Or, if you're into science fiction horror, the dead villain becomes a zombie and thereby produces a bigger threat than before. (3) The threat is eliminated, but that action reveals another threat that must be dealt with. For example, the villain dies or is killed, but only he had the formula for creating an antidote to a poison he had threatened to use, and it is stored in a laboratory or storage facility. That scenario can be the ending to a book with the potential for a sequel that may or may not ever get read by that reader. But the reader will still be content with the story, even if they're left hoping for a sequel.

Cliffhanger. (1) The plot does not resolve, and the reader must read the next book in the series to find out what happens. For example, in my (Randy's) book *F-S-H-S,* the second in my The Coded Message Trilogy, the wife of the main character, who has turned into a secondary main character, is kidnapped at the end of the book. Therefore, the main plot is not resolved. This almost forces the reader to go to the next book to get closure. Some readers may consider that "good investment," the term we stated earlier, because the ending is at such a high energy state they feel compelled to start the next book. Or it could cause some to be disappointed because they must take the next step and purchase another book to get the closure they desire. That is a trade-off that you as a writer must decide. Just remember, you won't be able to please all readers no matter your decision. (2) The eliminated threat or plot resolution has consequences, and those become the plot focus for the next book of the series. For example, the main character was able to diffuse a bomb that would have destroyed half the city, but now, because the bomb did not go off, another bomb is discovered that has been activated elsewhere. The next book of the series then addresses that subsequent crisis. This is somewhat related to number three in the previous paragraph. The major difference is that the previous example is a possible scenario that may occur, but in this example, it is a definite scenario that needs immediate attention. We would not suggest ending a series with this type of scenario, in which a threat is imminent, and no closure is provided. (3) The main plot is resolved, or satisfactorily resolved, to produce that "good investment" feel, but many subplots remain unresolved. This leaves the reader with nagging questions. This doesn't necessarily prevent the good investment feel, but it does leave the reader wanting closure. Just be sure that closure is finally resolved before the series is over.

As you can see, the possibilities are vast. Choose what works for you and the story you have created. Just don't forget about your readers and what will motivate them to continue your series. Keep them interested but not frustrated. Frustration will only make them stop and not finish, no matter if they never find out the answers they want. Granted, this is a fine line. And remember, you will not be able to please everyone. Do what you feel is best for your story. But also be aware that your publisher may have some say in this as well, as the professionals there have a good bit of experience with the genre and audience. They don't always step in, but they may.

Reviewing a bit, there are many factors that can contribute to which of these scenarios you choose, including: length of your novel, adding unpredictability to your storyline, how you have developed your storyline, and, of course, your own creativity. As C.S. Lewis said in the quote at the beginning of this chapter, your writing can create anything. (His own writing proved that.) But make what you write enjoyable for both yourself and your readers.

We would also like to point you to another resource you may find helpful: *The Story Template* by Amy Deardon. She has said that all stories follow a similar pattern, and she believes every story will, and should, follow this pattern for readers to enjoy. This can help you understand how to put your plot, or plots, together. Deardon dissects the storyline of many stories (books and movies) and finds a pattern.[8] Be aware of this pattern, but also don't let that decrease your creativity or the uniqueness of your story.

K * K * K * K * K * K * K

Tips and Information

From the Author

- **K**eep one overarching plot involving your main character.
- **K**eenly adding subplots can make a story more interesting, but plan and write these with clear organization. If not done carefully, this can add confusion to your readers.
- **K**now that all loose ends are resolved by the end of your story. Otherwise, readers will be frustrated.
- **K**ey to a story is its plot, and these can be as numerous and diverse as your imagination. Just be sure you bring your readers along, and end with a satisfactory resolution.

From the Editor

- **Keep a "story map"** by your side to track your plot, characters, subplots, and any correlating characters that arise with subplots. This can help greatly so you don't lose track of anything or anyone.

- **Know how to do a story map?** However you wish! Yellow legal pad off to the side, separate short document on your computer, or the proverbial corkboard with strings attached across the various elements the way detectives like to do. While that last example was tongue in cheek, do whatever works for you! (Do use more than a wadded-up piece of scrap paper to track your plots and characters, however.)

- **Knock out confusion.** If your plot even remotely confuses you as its author, or does so to your editor, you can be sure the reader is going to be confused.

- **Kneel to the bottom line** (of a different type): make sure your readers walk away with that "good investment" feeling. Even as the author, you can sense this. Write with this goal in mind.

Chapter 12

L

Live in the Moment

*"A bird doesn't sing because it has an answer;
it sings because it has a song."*
MAYA ANGELOU

Likely you are one of two types of writers. Either you are a meticulous planner of all aspects of your book, or you are a "pantser" (writing by the seat of your pants), one who develops and writes as you go along. (We'll get more into this aspect a little later in chapter *W: Ways of Writing*.) Either way, you need to have your readers live in the moment. As we have been saying, they need to be immersed in your story and feel they are nearly a part of it themselves.

How does one achieve this? For me (Randy), I envision I am the character I am currently writing about, so I ask myself the following: what would I say if someone said that to me? How would I react if someone did that, if I saw someone do that, or if I did that? *Become* your character at every moment in your story. This will keep your writing fresh, allow your readers to immerse themselves in your story, and make the characters nearly leap off the page and into real life.

Yet there is one major caution here: leave out unnecessary details. As you immerse yourself in a story, you will begin to visualize all the details. Let's do a little exercise here. Picture telling the following story by giving every detail listed here: the main character picks up the phone, punches the numbers, gets distracted by a package on the table, lays the phone down, opens the package, takes out the toy doll, remembers his daughter who died last year, breaks down and cries, reaches for a tissue, sees a newspaper headline which tells him the killer has struck again, runs out of the room, into his car, heads to talk to the reporter, and forgets about his phone still on the table. Now, would you write all of that? It would likely take several pages to do so. Is that a worthwhile investment in the story?

The answer: maybe yes, but likely no. You need to visualize all the minutiae, but you don't need to tell your reader every last piece of detail. You tell the major parts and let the reader's mind fill in the rest. That helps your reader become part of the creative process of your story. Here's a little secret: readers like to fill in the smaller details in their mind, even if they don't know it. Tell them all that is essential, but let them play with it a little in their mind as well.

Have you ever listened to two readers talk about the same book? While they have the same storyline, they usually fill in details totally differently. For example, the author may have written that a character had "beady eyes" without going into much detail. One would fill in what was not said this way: sallow complexion, somewhat gaunt, a sour disposition. Another would say the character had a rather round face, was somewhat on the pudgy side, and matter of fact in disposition. Why this difference? Because the author let the readers create the character in their minds as they felt best fit the story's scenario. Yet if the author gave away all the minutiae so that the reader needed zero creativity to envision the character, that reader may understand how the character looked but quite easily get distracted from the story's main plot. So it's better to ensure the storyline is not lost on the reader rather than provide too much small detail that one gets lost in to the point that they forget what they were caring about in the first place.

Now that is not to say there is no room for close detail. Sometimes the small details can build suspense. One can describe all the minor aspects of a room, its quietness, how all the creaks and groans can be heard, how the very dust creates an illusion of abandonment, and how the character can feel each beat of their heart. Does the reader need to know all this? Not really. At least, not from knowing about the room, but knowing how the look of the room makes the character feel. The close detail is driving the story and not detracting from the story. It is not simply a data dump, it is pulling the reader into the emotional state of the character. The reader is engrossed in the story and not distracted from it.

This difference is the key between a reader getting bored and inattentive to your story versus becoming absorbed in your story, feeling every heartbeat and thought of your character. The first is expulsion from your story. The second is total immersion in your story. Strive for the latter.

From the following two examples, see if you can tell which is a data dump and which captures the reader.

First example:

Sam entered the room. It seemed somewhat musty and cold. Dust was everywhere. The only piece of furniture likely worth salvaging was a sofa covered in plastic which was itself covered in a thick layer of dust. Everything about the room screamed nineteenth century: from the glass-bulbed lamps to the glass chandelier in the center of the vaulted ceiling. Only half the bulbs in the chandelier were lit thereby casting light and shadow haphazardly into the room and producing somewhat of an eerie ambiance. There, at the far end of the sofa, a blood stain on the carpet was still visible after all these years, the spot where his aunt had fallen, hitting her head on the end table. He closed his eyes remembering that awful phone call telling him his only living relative was no longer. Sam shook his head. He couldn't do it. He would pay someone else to clean out the house and resell. He stepped to the edge of the room, looked back once as he opened the front door, shook his head, and left.

Second example:

Sam entered the room. An odd feeling washed over him. He couldn't explain why, exactly, but being here made his skin prickle. He ran his finger over the corner of an end table yielding a thick coating of dust clinging to his finger, giving evidence to the passing of time since the death of his aunt in this very room. Her favorite sofa, now covered in plastic, and then in the same thick layer of dust, was likely the only thing he could salvage of her memory. The lights of the glass chandelier cast an eerie glow in the room as only half of the bulbs still burned as they cast a haphazard contrast of light and shadow to the room from its place in the center of the vaulted ceiling. It was as if time had passed and yet also ensured that the memory of the last day of his aunt's life was encased in a shrine of dust to mark that sad day. A nineteenth-century glass-bulbed lamp lay broken on the far end table with a glass shard next to a blood stain still visible in the carpet where his aunt had fallen, hitting her head on the corner of the table. His eyes teared and this throat constricted as if the very dust in the air was now suffocating him in the same way it had entombed this room, memorializing that awful day and the phone call he had received. He turned and left the room. He couldn't do it. He would pay someone else to clean out the house and resell. He looked back once he reached the door. He shook his head as a tear ran down his cheek. "Goodbye, Aunt Edna."

Did the two paragraphs read differently? Did the second one pull you into the story in a far more captivating way? It should have. While, yes, it may take a few more words to achieve this effect (the second paragraph has about half again as many words as the first), it definitely pays off in the end as readers become more engaged with the story.

Writing like this, they will likely stay with you until the end—and then wish there was more.

L*L*L*L*L*L

Tips and Information

From the Author
- Let yourself live in your characters' shoes as you write. This enables you to know the characters' proper reactions to whatever situations you place them in.

- Leave out unnecessary details. If it doesn't move your story along, it's likely not needed.
- Lift minutiae from your story unless it has the purpose of building suspense.

From the Editor

- Live in the moment: as a writer, strive for this goal. If you are living in the moment as you write, your readers will likely do the same.
- Less is sometimes more. You don't have to, or need to, show every detail. Make sure the ones you show have tangible purpose.
- Let your readers fill in some of the detail in their own minds; this will serve to help pull them into your story.

Chapter 13

M

Make Your Main Character Likeable

"Words are our most inexhaustible source of magic."
J. K. ROWLING

Maybe after everything we've said to here, this chapter's main thesis is already somewhat obvious. So we'll keep this M chapter necessarily short. To re-emphasize, however, your readers need to have an invested interest in your main character. That is what will allow them to stick with him or her and stay with that character through thick and thin until the very end. That means one of two things: they either like the main character, or they identify with the main character. Ideally, the reader does both.

This does not mean the main character has to be a saint and a hero combined in one. The main character can be plain vanilla. But there is a caveat with that statement. A certain ice cream commercial comes to mind. In one commercial, a company's vanilla bean ice cream is being pitched. How do they make plain vanilla sound sexy and appealing? They transform the viewers' expectations without changing the product. In the commercial, the man compares his girlfriend to the brand's vanilla ice cream. She is disappointed and feels this is actually a put-down. The guy then says something like: "Oh no. Not just any vanilla ice cream. A vanilla so potent you can find it in the dark." The lights go out and the woman gives an exaggerated, "Ooh." Viewers are led to believe there is something more special about this brand of vanilla than other brands. And now they're left wanting to try it.

That is what you want to do with your main character. The person can be plain, even to the point of boring. Yet you must make the reader feel there is something different about the character, or that something significant is going to happen to her or him. While the character may not change, the perception of the character must change for the reader to give their invested time and energy to the storyline.

Let's take the famed British writer C.S. Lewis and what may be his most famous work, *The Lion, the Witch, and the Wardrobe*. (Almost certainly you know the details of the story, but if you don't, or it's been years since you've read it, it's fast, fun reading.) Take the four main characters, the adolescent siblings Peter, Susan, Edmund, and Lucy Pevensie. At first introductions, they are quite unremarkable children, just as ordinary as their names. (I [Bob] often think Lewis wrote in these kinds of complexities, but that's another point for another time.) They're just four children displaced and living in the country, due to the war, with relatives they barely know. Nothing remarkable about them. But then Lucy, the youngest, stumbles onto a clothing wardrobe in an upper-level room of the house they're living in that . . . well, you know the rest of the story (quite likely, or most of it). The four go on a wonderfully remarkable journey that will change how they see everything.[9] The children are ordinary, but likeable, and you become deeply invested in what happens to them. This is a magical example of strong character building.

With this in mind, can you see the possibilities for your writing? Let's take, for the moment, the possibility that your main character is a villain. This can be the case, but this person can't be perceived as merely a villain. You must transcend the character or the perception of the character into something beyond the character's control so the reader remains invested. Perhaps the villain has some redeemable quality that sometimes peeks out at the reader. Perhaps the character is a villain because of something that happens to him or her makes the character become the villain so the reader can at least identify with the character's circumstances. They may not like the villain, but they can still identify with his or her motives that elicit the bad behavior. Perhaps they show some form of kindness despite their harshness—a peek at what the character could become. The reader will then want to find out if that glimmer of hope comes to fruition.

Remember, the story is important, but—have we said this before?—the reader is crucial. Without the reader, your story is in vain. It is sort of like the tree that falls in the forest when no one is around. Does it really make a noise? If your story has no reader, who does it enrich or transform?

M * M * M * M * M * M * M

Tips and Information

From the Author

- **M**anage your story to allow your readers to make an invested interest in your main character.
- **M**ainly, your readers should either like your main character or identify with them—ideally both.
- **M**ake your readers, even if the main character is a villain, want to follow him or her for investment reasons.

From the Editor

- **M**erge yourself, as the writer, to become one with your main character. Enjoy the writing process, and this will happen.
- **M**ake sure you have fun building characters! Use your life experiences to do so.
- **M**any well-written novels are at your disposal. Study some of the simple classics like Lewis's *The Lion, the Witch, and the Wardrobe* to see examples of strong character building.

Chapter 14

Number of Characters

"I write to give myself strength. I write to be the characters that I am not. I write to explore all the things I'm afraid of."
JOSS WHEDON

Now, there is no magic formula for the number of characters a story may need. You need to include as many as it takes to make your story complete, relatable, and interesting to your readers. (This is a chapter that will stick mostly with fiction novels and writing, not nonfiction, to make that clear from the start.) Amy Deardon, in her book *The Story Template*, says there are typically eight to ten characters that the reader gets to know and meet consistently, and she gives several examples of how she came to that conclusion.[10] However, this is not the total number of characters that will be in your story as you will also have a "supporting cast," so to speak. That would likely mean you will have approximately twenty to thirty characters in total. Sound like a lot? Overwhelming? Don't let it be. We think you'll find it won't be that difficult. Just remember what we have said a few times: put yourself in your story, and the number of characters needed will come to light.

Let us give two clear examples from the first book of three of Randy's The Coded Message Trilogy series and the first book of five of his Stele Prophecy Pentalogy series. Randy takes over a bit from here. The number of characters providing a point of view for these stories are quite different between the two, so they should make good examples to look at.

I (Randy) didn't try to make the number of characters in these books land in the range Deardon stated. Yet I'm curious if they did so. So I said to myself: let's find out.

In my first series, an astrophysicist working on a Mars mission uncovers a worldwide conspiracy related to this mission. In the first book of this series, *T-H-B*, the entire story is told from the perspective of the main character, Luke, the astrophysicist. While the storyline gets complicated, the point of view structure of the story is somewhat simple as you only get Luke's internal perspectives and thoughts that you as a reader can know. There are five other characters who are integral to the storyline: Sarah, a physician where Luke works and his love interest, their two friends (Jeremy, a famous restaurateur, and Natalia, an architect, both who Luke knew back in his college days), and two who become their friends (Oliver, a human resources consultant, and Viktoria, a trained soldier for an elite group called the Illumi-Alliance). These latter two at first appear to be against Luke but later become good friends. All six of these characters are dominant throughout the book as well as the series. But there are many other characters.

Luke and Sarah have work friends and coworkers who play a significant role in their work life: four for Luke (Scott and Brian, his fellow astrophysicists; Larry, his supervisor; and Dwayne, a propulsion specialist) and three for Sarah (Kathleen, the head nurse at the aerospace center; Ken, her supervisor; and Bruce, a lawyer and past love interest). But there are two additional people who both Luke and Sarah get to know well (Jason, an event planner for the aerospace engineering center, and Jared, his partner who becomes a physical health trainer at the company).

Then let's not forget about the villains. There are six of those, one per continent (as the storyline has it), since this is a story about a worldwide conspiracy (Doctors Rozencrantz, Cortês, Mercure, Li, Meriwether, and the Supreme Oracle, who are all involved in some way with the Mars mission Luke is working on and members of this elite group, the Illumi-Alliance), with one of these becoming a major character. And then there are two characters who are somewhat like go-betweens who work for the villains but end up becoming friends of Luke and some of his friends, with one of them becoming a major character in this book (Oracle Tatum, a leader of invocation ceremonies in Houston, and Marta, a maker of invocation wafers in Rome who later becomes a chef).

Also, there are six characters, somewhat minor, who contribute to subplots (René and Philippe Mauchard, Caine, Abel, Valerie, and Anton), all of whom are involved or connected with the Illumi-Alliance in some way. One of these, Philippe, becomes a major villain, so to speak, in the second and third books of this series where you see things from his point of view for a time as the story plot thickens in the final two books. Of course, there are "extras" who perform some function, or who these other characters interact with, but the reader hardly gets to know them at all.

So how many characters does that make? I count twenty-nine in total, with eight of them being major characters. So this book seems to fall within the parameters Deardon outlined. Now, while that sounds like a lot, don't worry. The reader can easily comprehend this number of characters and not become confused.

Now let's see if this holds true for another of my books.

The first book of my Stele Prophecy Pentalogy series, *Mercy of the Iron Scepter*, is different from the previous book we just discussed as it has several subplots which require the reader to understand several character points of view. You will see this is achievable, but you as the writer must be careful to let your readers know whose point of view you are providing—especially when several of the characters who you provide points of view for are in scenes together, and only one character's point of view can be provided per scene.

This book is about an archaeologist trying to vindicate his brother, who rebelled against the King almost fourteen years earlier, by trying to accurately decipher a prophecy from certain stone steles he uncovers. There are two main characters: Kalem, the archaeologist trying to solve the prophecy, and Angela, his pseudo love interest and the person key to the prophecy Kalem is trying to solve. Both are provided with points of view to the reader because, while they are attracted to each other, Kalem is against the King, but Angela is for the King. I thought it important for readers to understand their internal struggles with this aspect of their relationship.

Two of Kalem's friends (Robert and Dillon) become key characters, as well as two people close to Angela (Raina, her adopted mother, and Peter, her stepbrother). Because of other subplots, both Robert and Raina are given points of view for the readers. This is done with Robert because he is a close friend of Kalem's but becomes a follower of the King even while helping Kalem. Raina is also a follower of the King, but she has a big role in uniting many of the characters in the story. So it was important for readers to understand their internal struggles as well.

Then these characters become involved with two additional individuals (Mik'kel and Edvin, who are close friends of each other and with Raina, with Edvin becoming a major character). Because of the backdrop of this story, there are four characters of a heavy spiritual type who become major in the storyline (Shepherds Franklin and Benjamin, who teach scripture, and angels Azel and Uriel, who befriend Angela). To better understand the larger picture, I felt it important to know the internal struggles of Shepherd Franklin as well to enhance readers' appreciation of this unique world and how these characters interact with each other.

Kalem then meets three other individuals who become major characters: Jenkins, someone who helps him uncover two of the steles he is searching for; Ilana, who works with Robert; and Melana, who works with Angela and becomes a love interest for Peter.

There are fourteen individuals who are not major characters, but slightly more than minor, who do significant things that propel the plot forward: Harcaine, who leads the analyses of the steles Kalem is seeking; Tiberius, who heads the Jerusalem Science Center; Janet, Kalem's mother; the Overtaker, of whom the stele prophecy is about; Marguerite and Pablo, who work with Peter; Saulo, who works with the

Overtaker; Eldridge, the keeper of the King's agenda; the King, the leader of the world; Shepherds Randall, Morgan, Carlos, and Vadik, who also teach scripture and befriend Kalem; and Alexei, who works with Shepherd Vadik.

I also allowed readers to understand some of the internal thoughts of the character entitled the Overtaker as he is the main antagonist of the story. So, in all, six characters have points of view at various times in the storyline so readers can better understand the subplots of the story. This helps you see a story structure can become complicated, but you can write it so it doesn't confuse your readers as long as you are clear regarding whose point of view you are presenting at any one time.

The total number of significant characters comes to (also) twenty-nine (I certainly didn't plan that) with ten of them being major characters. So this book, even though more complicated in structure than the previous one, also holds true to the character paradigm as mentioned by Deardon.

One of the larger points is this: don't get too hung up on the number of characters needed. As you can see in these two examples, just by me working through these stories as I wrote them, the right number of characters came to light and fit into the paradigm presented. This will likely happen for you as well. Yet don't let this be a hang-up for your writing. You as the author will determine how many characters are needed to propel your story forward.

At the same time, don't ignore this either. Count the number after you get through your first rough draft. See if it fits this range. If not, do a simple thing: ask yourself why. You may have a good reason for fewer characters than this typical number, or you may have more than this number. Just be careful about going with more, as this can create the potential for your story to become confusing for your readers as they may not be able to keep track.

From both of us: a quick word here. It takes an extraordinarily practiced and veteran author to come up with scores and scores of characters, even more than a hundred. We think of Dostoevsky and *The Brothers Karamazov*. Don't try to write to that level—at least early in your career. That's genius level writing, and not many (certainly not us!) are capable of that kind of skill and detail.

Fewer is likely less of an issue, but the story must be extraordinarily strong and compelling if you go with much fewer than the range quoted here. If you have fewer, check to see if you need to create more interest to your story with some less significant characters.

In summary, once again, this is just a guide. Don't let it become restrictive for your writing, but liberating, as it can help ensure you are on the right track.

N * N * N * N * N * N * N

Tips and Information

From the Author
- **Normally, a story will have eight to ten characters the readers get to know well.**

- Naturally, many characters will have only a supporting role in your story and be only a part of the twenty to thirty characters in total.

- Navigating the number of characters will not become difficult if you put yourself into your story as you write.

- Now, if your first draft contains more or less than the optimum number of characters, simply ask why. You may be able to justify the number you have used.

From the Editor

- Never lose track of your characters, and introduce them well the first time. Similar to other tips: keep a side notepad on your characters, or side computer file, something helpful of this nature.

- Note when characters appear in your story. If a large gap of time (or number of pages) has passed, make shorter but clear references back to who this person was when first introduced. It's easy for a reader to remember little about a person introduced, say, eight chapters or ninety pages earlier.

- Nothing is quite as annoying as when an author is not consistent with things like spellings, how characters talk, information about them in succeeding appearances, and other things of this nature. As an example: if a side character, who is no longer having children when you first introduced her, has three offspring, please don't give her four when she comes back into the story the next time.

Chapter 15

O

Overwhelm
(Don't Do It to Your Readers)

*"I can shake off everything as I write;
my sorrows disappear, my courage is reborn."*
ANNE FRANK

Obviously, you want to inspire your readers, maybe even wow them. But you don't want to overwhelm them. That just makes them shut down and not want to move forward with your story. You want your readers to hate to put your book down, not hate to pick it up. There are several things that may tend to overwhelm your readers, so keep these in mind, in a big-picture way, as you write.

The first is to *avoid long paragraphs*. Have you ever turned a page and there was hardly any white space or breaks through the entire new page? Be honest: what went through your mind?

Did you say to yourself, "Oh wonderful! An extremely long paragraph!"? Likely not. A mental groan likely went through your mind knowing this was something you'd have to plow through—or possibly choose to skip. You definitely don't want your readers skipping through your text. You want them riveted to every word.

Granted, there are times you need to provide a lot of information, but there are also creative ways to accomplish this without a massive data dump. When possible, keep your paragraphs on the short side, and many of them flat-out short. Sometimes that is achieved just by breaking a first-written long paragraph into smaller paragraphs. It's the same information but looks far more appealing without producing that mournful, mental sigh.

Even better, dole the information out to your readers in small packets dispersed between dialogue or action scenes. That way you can give just enough information to yield clarity to what is occurring without making your readers learn something they will need to remember a long time from a data dump, or even forget what was occurring prior to a data dump. (And, in truth, a data dump is something you pretty much want to avoid.) Providing information piecemeal will, more times than not, be preferred.

The next tip is to *avoid words for words' sake*. Make every word count. If a word is not needed, don't use it. If the information is not crucial to the reader, they will tire of it, and easily. Remember, they are not as tied to your story as you are. Of course, you want them to be, but you must create strong reasons for the reader to care about your story. So choose your words wisely and carefully. Create the tension, the flow, you want your readers to feel. Words are powerful. Use them to their fullest potential.

One of the best ways to know if you have accomplished this is to give the story a breather after you've written a section. When you come back, if you get bored from parts of your story, this by itself is not a bad thing: you are getting in tune with your writing—and your readers. You may feel the information is critical, but you need to make sure your readers feel this as well. If they start skipping over parts they consider boring, they may miss some vital information they need later to understand your storyline. Then they'll be lost, which only leads to your readers being more overwhelmed. This then leads to disinterested readers who eventually never finish your story. And, unfortunately, that may lead to those readers not taking a chance on other books you have written.

There are plenty of other creative things you can do to avoid overwhelming either yourself or your readers. *Reading the writing of other authors* helps you see how they write and express themselves. Doing this will likely stir up more ideas in your mind on how to write something just a little differently to help your creation always feel fresh to your readers. *Attending a writing conference* can yield great ideas as well, and maybe you will inspire others.

More tips: *study your craft, learn better grammar, and learn how to say something in more than one way.* Remember our G chapter: you don't always have to use proper grammar, but you should know when you have chosen not to . . . and why.

Always have purpose behind every word and sentence you write.

Let us provide one famous example of most of the ideas mentioned in the last three paragraphs, particularly reading other authors and studying your craft. When I (Bob) started in publishing, early on I got my hands on Stephen King's *On Writing*, a sort of writing memoir of his work in the industry. King, the famous writer of terror genre and *The Shawshank Redemption* author. One of the most famous American authors of the last half-century, right? I was blown away to read King write that, through the years, *reading* has been a crucial part of his writing day. He writes that, "It's what I do at night, kicked back in my blue chair."[11] I would imagine he still does this, or something close, to this day.

Write with purpose, with conviction, with passion, and not to overwhelm.

Two more great references on this topic are William Strunk Jr. and E. B. White's book, *The Elements of Style* and William Zinsser's *On Writing Well*. (Both are a few decades old now, but to show how principles are timeless, that doesn't matter in the least. They are million-plus bestsellers, and absolute gold to learn more about strong writing. They are listed in our resources section at the end of the book.) They have more information that will help you avoid the "overwhelming" aspects we've just discussed. They have many examples of what and what not to do. These two classics are not by any means a must before you can begin writing, but both are excellent tools to continue turning to in one's writing arsenal.

O * O * O * O * O * O

Tips and Information

From the Author

- **O**verarching thought: you want your readers hating to put your book down.
- **O**rient your text so you have no long paragraphs or "data dumps."
- **O**bserve how other writers write; this will stir up your own ideas.
- **O**nly write like you, and not like anyone else. Again, though, you do need to know and be able to justify why you have written as you have.

From the Editor

- **O**mit long paragraphs: the first sight of them is often tiring to a reader. There are times to justify them, but you don't want many.
- **O**ld but good advice followed by many editors and writers: read your sentences out loud, to yourself, in front of the computer. See how they sound. If you can hear a long, winding nature or a verbose passage that only slows things down, make changes.
- **O**ften said, and yet still great words to follow: Read, read, read other authors.

Chapter 16

P

Point of View

"Difficulties mastered are opportunities won."
WINSTON CHURCHILL

Planning for which point of view you want to incorporate into your story is important. We've talked about some aspects of point of view earlier in chapter *F: Flavor of Writing*. Let's explore the topic a little more in-depth.

There are four main points of view (also called POV) a writer can consider: first person, second person, third person limited, and third person omniscient. Here are important things to consider about each.

First person. It is as if the writer is a character in her or his own story. If done well, it can allow you a deeper connection with your readers, as if you and your readers are sitting together, and you are telling them a story about yourself and what occurred. The story and what can be conveyed is limited to only what you as a character know, and thus it will be from a biased point of view. Readers know only what the character knows or thinks and will have to decide if they believe what is being told them rather than knowing for certain what the truth may actually be. Some may find that enjoyable, others not.

Look at books in your favorite reading genre and see if this is the typical point of view used. When readers are hooked to a certain genre, they expect—and like—things a certain way. That is not to say you can't change things up. After all, someone always has to be first. But, as we have said before, better you know that you are changing things up than to do so ignorantly. Again, be purposeful in all you do and write. Nothing is off limits, necessarily, but better to know where you are than to realize you have painted yourself into a corner you didn't expect to be in.

Because you can only present what one character is thinking, things are somewhat limited in what can be conveyed to a reader. We have seen some novels where the author overcame this by having different chapters delivered from the first-person perspective of different characters by indicating in the chapter title whose perspective is being presented. This allows the reader a greater perspective to the plot of the story and to know the truth of the bias of the characters, giving deeper insight into the entire storyline you the author are trying to present. This shows that knowing the strengths and weaknesses of a point of view can give you, the writer, the opportunity to use both to their fullest extent.

Second person. While this has been used successfully, it is more uncommon, likely because you are placing your reader as a character in your story. This point of view is almost certainly the riskiest of the four. Some readers may find it extremely engaging, as it does immerse the reader directly into the story—after all, they have become part of it. (On the other hand, this means it had better be a particularly strong story to hold their interest.) Others, however, are adamantly against this. Again, know what you are doing and why you are doing it.

You can also consider utilizing this point of view within another point of view. For example, perhaps one character has a dream about another. When the dream is conveyed, you can switch to a second person point of view. This can allow a deeper connection between the dream and the reader and, perhaps, provide a greater impact than just conveying the events of the dream. Your readers would then not feel they are the character but would place themselves in the dream as the other character. A closer, more intimate connection could be established between the story of the dream and your readers, but your readers would not feel they are being told how they are feeling through the experience.

Third person limited. This point of view has something in common with first person as both allow an increased level of intimacy with your reader. In both, readers can know what the character is thinking and feeling. What this point of view can do that first person cannot is that you can have more than one character from whom the reader is drawing on their perspective. Not at the same time, of course, but you can be inside a different character in different scenes and thus give the reader a greater perspective and allow him or her a connection to more than just one character.

Now, we stated how this can be done using first person. The main difference here is that this can be done without having to actually tell the reader whose perspective is being presented, as this will become clear within the story itself. While the reader can only know what the character presented at the time knows, it allows the intricacies of the story to be revealed as the character knows about them. So the reader can be surprised when the character is surprised or feel sorrow when the character feels sorrow. In this manner the reader is not prepared ahead of time and can feel the full brunt of emotion along with the character. This can create quite a powerful connection between your characters and your readers.

Third person omniscient. This point of view uses the same pronouns as with third person limited, but here all is known. It can be used quite successfully for providing backstory, but be careful you don't allow this to become a data dumping ground. Rather than engaging your reader, this may do the opposite. This technique essentially allows you as the author to become a character in your story as the narrator. You are connecting to your reader directly and not necessarily through the character. You allow the reader to not be limited in knowing only what one character at a time knows but what you know, which is, simultaneously, everything.

Please note, this is not the same thing as head-hopping, which we discussed under chapter *H: Head-Hopping Should Be Avoided*. Here, you as the writer have become a person in your story as the narrator, and you have established a rapport with your reader. This technique, though, can distance your reader from your characters as you, as the narrator, are connecting with your reader and not necessarily the character or characters of your story. While the same information may be getting to your reader, it is by quite different techniques. You, the narrator, are providing information rather than the character. You may have told what the character is thinking, but the character didn't convey that to the reader, so that does create some distance and a decreased level of intimacy between the character and the reader.

Again, this can be combined with other points of view. For example, you may use third person omniscient in the beginning of your story to connect with readers by introducing and providing information about your main character so your readers know some necessary background information ahead of time: something about the town, the customs of the day, or anything, really, that will prepare your readers for your story. You can also do this periodically throughout your story to condense a long time frame into just a few sentences. Just be careful that you don't go so far that you lose your reader. Remember, they are reading for entertainment; they are not wanting to be forced to form a Vulcan mind meld with you for all the information you know.

In summary, you have a number of options at your disposal, but choose wisely. Don't use one over the other just because it would be different, but because it will elicit the response you want from your readers. Again, doing something different is fine, but do it for a reason that will propel your story, grab your readers, and keep them glued to your work from start to finish. All are acceptable as long as you know the reason you are using the techniques you have chosen.

Words are powerful tools. Use them like a skilled craftsman uses his tools to make a one-of-a-kind piece of furniture. One in which everyone who experiences it comes away feeling at least a little grateful (if not a lot) that they had the encounter.

* * * * *

Print Out Portions and Read Them Aloud

Perhaps this is one of the most simple of our tips, and yet one we promise will help you: don't be satisfied with simply reading on the screen. Print selected portions of your manuscript and sit with them somewhere else. Even, as said in the tips box in the previous chapter, read out loud. You'll be amazed what that brings to life, what jumps out at you.

Sit in your reading chair; that's a comfortable space anyway, right? You love to sit and read there and feel comfort in doing so. If you're sitting in that same space, reading your own work, and wincing a bit . . . good! You've learned something. Writing is all about learning the craft as we go. Read it again. Pretty sure that could be written a bit better, right? Highlight however you want, then go back and do so later.

Will that take a little more time? Yes. Will you eventually thank yourself? Also yes.

Do you have to do this with every word you write? No. That's a lot of printing! But does it help to do this with sections you're being extra careful with or those that somehow just don't "feel right" in your mind? Yes to both questions. In short, use this trick as much as you need. You'll feel more confident in those difficult areas of your writing.

P * P * P * P * P * P * P

Tips and Information

From the Author

- **P**otentially, if done well, writing in first person point of view can provide a more intimate connection to your readers, yet know that it is limited in what can be conveyed to your readers.

- **P**lacing your reader as a character in your story by writing in second person can be engaging but is much more difficult, and it is uncommon.

- **P**robably the most common point of view is writing in third person limited because it allows you to give more than one character's point of view, although not at the same time.

- **P**ossibly the best point of view for backstory or scene setting is third person omniscient. This point of view allows you as the author to become a character in your story, one who functions as a narrator.

From the Editor

- **P**oints of view switched randomly between characters will only distract and confuse your readers, so this is almost certainly something you want to avoid.

- **P**robably, third person-limited or third-omniscient are better choices of POV if you're new at writing or still working on learning more basic elements of the craft.
- **P**rint out selected versions of your manuscript; this gives a rough feeling of sitting and holding a book. It also gives you a more objective eye toward your work. Also very helpful: read sections of your writing in a different space than where you usually do. Take your laptop to another room or, say, your back porch, and read aloud.

Chapter 17

Q
Question Why
(Yet Answer with a Positive)

"Write your first draft with your heart. Rewrite with your head."
MIKE RICH

Quell those fears about becoming a writer that are rising within you. Thoughts like: *do I have it in me to actually be a writer?* Suppress them.

We know we're putting a lot of information out there with this book. Thinking that you must attend to everything can be daunting. But the point of this little two-book series is to be comprehensive, not overwhelming. Take it in small chunks. So let's go back to the question: *can you really be a writer?*

Well of course you can be a writer! That's the good news. Anyone and everyone should write. That doesn't mean you'll be published by your dream publisher, become famous, or be the next great American, or international, novelist. But you *should* write.

It's therapeutic. It's cleansing. It frees the mind.

All those things comprise the good news. Now for the other side: *why* do you want to be a writer?

From Bob: once while in a newspaper managers' workshop (a former career, a former lifetime, I like to say) the instructor talked about how newspapers were published daily (and, at the time, still popular). Becoming a reporter and gathering news can be difficult, he was saying, but one eventually gets there through perseverance. In the end, that sheer process can prove rewarding.

He then made a point in the form of a question: do you, as a newsroom editor, enjoy sitting down merely to write? I'll never forget his answer to his own question. "I'd rather dig a ditch on a hot day than write, to be honest," he said.

Now his statement was likely a bit of an exaggeration, unless that man actually enjoyed the back-breaking work of slinging dirt (which he probably didn't). His point: writing is hard. It doesn't flow easily. Writers who can bang out five thousand words a day with hardly a sweat are the Beethovens of their craft. They're rarities, savants. Writing for the rest of us? Writing is labor. Writing takes much thought. Writing takes putting yourself out there. Writing commits you (if you're at all serious) to rounds and rounds of work and rework on the same passages.

This is a starting point: does your why include your willingness to persevere? Know why you want to write.

But let's dive a little deeper.

There is another why: know why you write the *words* you do. We've mentioned this before but want to emphasize it here. Be sure you know the why behind everything you do. Some of this will become second nature over time, but this is a question you should continuously ask—no matter your writing experience.

We would say not to worry too much about this aspect in your first draft, as this is when you are letting your creativity flow and getting your ideas down on the computer, or on paper, or at least out of your head. Yet when you go over your work, or you are self-editing, continuously ask yourself *why*.

Let's make this a little easier, because, at the same time, it's challenging. You don't have to spend hours on these questions. Just kick them around a bit in your head. Ask yourself these simple questions and answer with simple answers. This small exercise alone (asking and answering at least some of the questions below) can sharpen portions of your writing.

Some of the questions:

1. Why did I write this section this way?

2. Does this section read as I want it to, or as it needs to read?

3. Is my intent clear?

4. Could this section be written better, clearer, more like this character would act, or closer to how this character would speak?

5. Do the words used convey the tone I want them to carry?

6. Do I use the same word repeatedly in sequential sentences? In the same sentence (even worse)? (Articles like *a* or *the* are not included in that test, nor simple words/ most prepositional words like *to* or *as*.)

7. Does the flow of the content seem natural, or is it stilted?

As you can see, there are a number of these simple questions to ask yourself. As we said, at first glance this can seem overwhelming. But again, don't let it be. The overarching question is: *why did I use the words I chose?* All other questions stem from there.

While this is a short chapter, we feel this understanding is a vital component to strong writing. You as the author are the creator of your work, your story. Therefore, you should be able to defend, if needed, all aspects of your story to a reader, or to anyone who questions a section of your work. You wrote it. Now defend why you wrote as you did. In the end, it's all about writing with purpose.

So yes, write with purpose, write with clarity, write with enthusiasm, and know the why behind your words.

Q * Q * Q * Q * Q * Q * Q

Tips and Information

From the Author

- Quality is important. Anyone can be a writer, yet not everyone can be a good writer without studying how to write. (Your reading this book is an excellent part of that study!)
- Question yourself and know why you want to be a writer.
- Qualify your writing by knowing the why behind each section of your story and why you presented each section the way you did.

- **Quota** (or trying to crank out a certain number of words per day/week/month) is secondary: write with purpose, write with clarity, write with enthusiasm, and know the why behind your words.

From the Editor

- **Query** the reason you are writing, and the passion you have behind what you want to say, and the internal whys will answer themselves far more easily.

- **Quench** your doubts. Those whys about the choices you make are important! Ask the questions. If you know where you're going with your overall purpose, the questions will eventually answer themselves.

- **Quill** to paper, or fingertips to keys, writing is hard work—if you're going to do it with any degree of seriousness. There's no such thing as sitting down for a half-hour and banging out a thousand wonderfully crafted words. We will need to plan a bit, write, write some more, self-edit, and rewrite again. Your motivations are going to need to keep driving you.

Chapter 18

Reality of Characters

*"If the book is true, it will find an audience
that is meant to read it."*
WALLY LAMB

Recognize how your characters come across to your readers. Are they real or phony? This is an important concept to realize, and something a good writer needs to master. We talked in an earlier chapter about getting your readers to like, or at least understand, your main characters. This short chapter adds a bit to that concept.

You will likely need characters who are not likeable but are important to your story. Yet the person, the character, must still feel real. This partly goes back to the previous chapter of asking yourself why: why did you make this character in this fashion? Is this the way someone of this type of personality and background would act, react, and speak? Understand your characters.

How do you do this? One way is to immerse yourself in your story. Pretend you are in the middle of it. You should not be at a high level, looking down on your story and writing what you see. You should be enveloped in your story. You are placing yourself into the heart of each character as you show what is happening. This will allow what is being done, said, felt, and portrayed to seem real to your reader, because these actions are real to you, the character involved in your story.

Let's add one thing: this rule would apply (as most in this book) whether you are writing a novel, some other kind of fiction, or historical fiction (a popular genre); and in nonfiction with sections that employ fictional characters to make various points, or even actual people you are writing about in your nonfiction to make your point. In the latter case, the person you are writing about *still* needs to read like a real person!

(Side point, but an organizational one: you must ask the actual person their permission for use, or you must carefully keep them from being identified through your work if they don't wish to be used or you can't reach them.)

In any of these cases, your people need to be real. This is a fairly simple guideline to follow, so this makes this short chapter a relatively easy one! Some ways to do this:

- Read your section out loud. Would my character say those words *in that way?*
- Visualize the actual motion: she walked to the roofline in her high heels and precariously peered over the edge. Would she actually do that? Maybe she would! Maybe that's the point of the scene. But make sure it's real.

- And last—we'll have more to say about this in this book and the companion book on self-editing—have reader-friends (and experts in this field who you know) take a look at your book, or at least read through a section or sections you're not sure about. You'll want outside readers even before you get to your editor. Those readers may be wrong on some points, or offer what is not very good or clear advice (because they may not know writing as well as you!), but they almost certainly will point out some things that will prove useful in some areas.

Now, don't confuse this with the head-hopping rule we spoke about earlier. You as the author are head-hopping (but only in your mind) so you can write from an intimate part of your story. Yet you are not making the reader head-hop. Your readers are viewing the story from one character's point of view. (Refer to chapter *P: Point of View* for more on this topic.)

The more real your characters feel to your reader, the more likely your reader will be glued to your story. And that is the best compliment any reader can give: *I felt like I was a part of your story. It all seemed so real.*

That will put a spring in those fingers at the keyboard!

R*R*R*R*R*R*R

Tips and Information

From the Author

- **Remember**, your characters should feel real to your readers.
- **Real** and identifiable: this is how your characters should come across to your readers. This is achieved by immersing yourself in your story.
- **Readers** should never be forced to head-hop through your characters, even though you as the author can, and should, head-hop (in your mind) between characters as you write.
- **Rest** assured, the best compliment any reader can give an author is, "I felt I was a part of your story. It all seemed so real."

From the Editor

- **Realness** of characters can be achieved through the three ways listed in this chapter. This doesn't need to take all day; you can apply the first two simple tests quite easily.
- **Rely** on your judgment and trust your gut! (Your gut plus, perhaps, what your reader-friends have said, assuming they are giving sound advice.) If you think the

character would say that phrase in exactly *that* way, or do that action, great. Leave it in place.

- **R**ework your words, or the action, or both if your character fails a realness test. You're going to do lots of reworking anyway, so don't be surprised or discouraged. Enjoy the writing process!

FOUR

The Most Important Rule of Writing? Here It Is

Chapter 19

Show, Don't Tell

> *"No tears in the writer, no tears in the reader. No surprise in the writer, no surprise in the reader."*
> ROBERT FROST

Study and memorize this chapter title, for if you haven't heard the phrase, it is one you will hear repeatedly as you continue to learn, study, and teach yourself the writing craft. But what does it really mean? It means you are showing, or describing, the emotion rather than just stating the emotion.

By the way, this writing rule—so important we've made it a section unto itself—will often supplement, and make flow, many of our other guidelines by itself. For instance, the preceding chapter about realness of characters. Following this guideline will take you a long way toward meeting that one.

So what does it mean to show, don't tell? An example:

Tell: Mary entered the room and saw the surprise on Jayne's face. Evidently, Jayne wasn't expecting her to arrive so early.

Show: Mary entered the room. Jayne's eyes grew wide, and her jaw dropped as her hand flew to her chest with a gasp. "Mary! I . . . I wasn't expecting you for another hour!"

Now which of those versions did you like the best? Of course it was the second one, right? But why? (Again: ask the *why* question.)

With the second version you are better able to view Jayne's reaction. It just feels more real, as though you are in the room watching her reaction. Your perspective changed as well, most likely. While both versions are from Mary's perspective, the second version allows you to better understand what is going on with Jayne at the same time (again, even though written from Mary's point of view). This version allows you to connect better with Jayne than does the first version.

Also, it's usually the case that the number of words increases when you show and don't tell. In this example, the word count for showing is more than one and a half the number of telling (34 words versus 20). While this use of words may increase your word count, it is still well worth your time. Your readers will benefit. Will this make your text become too voluminous? Not necessarily. Check out chapter *U: Unnecessary Words.*

Show, don't tell is more than just describing emotion. It can be used during dialogue to let your reader determine the characteristics of a person, what they think, and how they react to what is going on around them. It brings your reader into your story much better than merely telling them about a character.

We know some of you are likely saying: yes, but I need to get to the action scene quickly. I don't have time for a lot of telling. We hear you. Sometimes you can compromise and give your reader both. Provide a short description of action to propel your story forward so you can keep your cadence and momentum at the same time. You can choose some strong action words to accomplish this. While the shorter choice may not give an entirely detailed picture of the scene to your reader, it will provide enough for them to paint a mental snapshot as they rapidly get to the action.

Here are examples of effective use of show, don't tell. Both can be useful; the second is a shorter-word choice that might help you better move your pacing.

Detailed showing: The air was crisp as Jake hurried down the narrow trail between the tall, majestic pecan trees. He turned up his collar to brace against the cold trying to seep through his overcoat. This caused him to increase his pace even more as he needed to arrive at the cottage at the end of the trail. At the moment, the small house looked like a faint glow that appeared to twinkle as wind gusts caused bare tree limbs to blow back and forth against the vision of his destination. Although the coldness made his breath visible with each pant of his quickened pace, it blew away in a flash with each gust of wind. This effect caused him to press on ever more quickly. It was paramount Jake reach his ill wife before her breath was forever clipped short from her frail frame.

Short showing: The air was crisp, the wind cold as Jake increased his pace down the long, lonely trail of majestic trees that led to his ill wife. He just had to get to the cottage before she would take her final breath. His breath, initially visible from the coldness but then disappearing in a flash with each gust of cold, was a constant reminder hers could be cut short forever— at any moment. He saw the twinkle of cabin light ahead in the distance. He put his head down and pressed on; time was of the essence.

While the long showing version provides more elements and creates a more detailed picture, the shorter version gets the reader to Jake's destination faster yet still creates the same mood and urgency. There is nothing wrong with the first version, and it can be used. The choice of the shorter or longer version is a choice you make concerning how you intend to lead your reader and what experience you want for them. Perhaps Jake's journey to get to his ill wife is more important in terms of his inner dialogue, and you could have various thoughts go through his mind to help your reader understand something about him as he handles this crisis. But if what is to occur after he reaches his ill wife is more important for the reader, then the second may be more appropriate. It still conveys the emotion and allows the reader visual cues to build the scene but quickly takes her or him to the important point you want your reader to experience. (Last, a word count comparison: the first has 143 words, the second 96. Which is better? In this case, it's the one that best serves your reader and overall purpose.)

Now, does this mean you should always use the show, don't tell technique rather than just quickly stating the emotion or action? No. Remember what we have said. Be purposeful in what you do. If you don't use this technique in each instance, know why you didn't. There are times when the emotion of a scene is not key to the story or not needed to elicit an emotion in your reader. That is certainly okay and a reason for not showing the emotion. Just be sure you know you did not use the technique and *why* you didn't.

Each of these chapters provides guidance and will apply much to most of the time. Yet there is no rule that is absolute. You are the architect of your work. Use your words to wield your magic on your audience.

A great exercise is this: try writing detailed, and shorter (two writings, as we did above), show-not-tell sections. We'll provide a starter, perhaps, for you:

> *Will is late to his subway stop in a semi-crowded station. The doors will close soon, he notices, ever hurrying. As he approaches his train, out of the corner of his eye, he notices a man accosting a woman with verbal, if not physical—he isn't yet sure what he saw—abuse. Will has to make a decision...*

Have fun writing two show-don't-tell descriptions of this scene.

One more word of caution. Be sure you don't use the same words and phrases for an emotion that may repeatedly occur. This could be one reason for not showing all emotions, as you will need to vary your techniques to not become repetitive. Also, learn synonyms you can use to show the same emotion in different ways so things do not read repetitively even though the emotion itself may be repetitive.

At the bottom is this: to "tell" is wooden. To "show" is... to draw the reader in, to make them a part of the story. Readers can sense a difference. They won't stop reading after a few wooden lines, but they will if it continues for pages and pages. We've done it many times.

Here is one resource you can utilize to get ideas for how to show various emotions: *The Emotion Thesaurus: A Writer's Guide to Character Expression* by Angela Ackerman and Becca Puglisi (also listed in our Resources at the back). You'll find this a useful text to bring your writing to a new level of professionalism.

* * * * *

Stick to the Main Thing

Such a simple thing, and we're going to keep it that way here. And yet, so important. Make virtually everything you do support your main storyline. Have you ever read a book in which the author has gotten so far afield—three, four side issues away from the main—that it was literally tiring? *When is this going to return to the main situation with Bryson? What are we doing over here, now?* These types of thoughts can be common.

I (Bob) want to provide a quick example of a series of books with many subplots, and yet they all tie well together. In Randy's Erabon Prophecy trilogy (the books are *Myeen, Sharab,* and *Qerach*), everything follows the main character, named (actually, nicknamed) Nuke. He's an astronaut in a future point of time in which space exploration has led to the outer parts of the solar system. An accident happens, and Nuke's craft is flung through an interstellar gate into a different solar system in a different galaxy. From there, our main character finds six different planets, all tied together in various cultural ways, but also splintered from each other in a constant state of distrust if not near-war. As you might imagine just from reading those few sentences, Randy introduces dozens of characters (and the books aren't that long!), all with strong detail. And yet . . . everything comes back to, and stays with, Nuke. His journey. His efforts to try to get home. Finding himself and his purpose while trying to get home. (I found Randy's ending to this short but somewhat complex series satisfying and particularly well done. No, it didn't provide a happy-happy conclusion. But it just . . . worked.) There are many branches, but everything stays with Nuke's journey. So . . . stick to the main thing.

S * S * S * S * S * S * S

Tips and Information

From the Author

- **Show** the emotion using description rather than just telling the emotion.
- **Showing** and not telling makes the story and characters feel more real.
- **Strive** to balance detail versus action.
- **Stand** as the architect of your work. Use your words to wield your magic on your audience.

From the Editor

- **Search** for the right times to show, not tell. While you cannot do this with every sentence, or paragraph, often you can. This simple rule is one of the golden ones of writing.
- **Showing** versus telling will yield higher word counts in most cases, and yet the overall effect is worth it. As

your writing gets crisper, the net effect is greater. You will set the scene in a stronger way and perhaps not need as many words in a following scene.

- **S**tyle is an important aspect of your writing: it should be engaging to your readers versus sounding wooden or stiff. If a few sentences you have written bore you, imagine the reaction of your readers.
- **S**tick with your main storyline. As stated in the second 'S' in this chapter (Stick to the Main Thing), don't drift too far afield. Make everything you write support your main storyline (fiction) or thesis (nonfiction).

FIVE

Write for You? Yes. Write for Your Readers? Also Yes.

Chapter 20

Tense

"To produce a mighty book, you must choose a mighty theme."
— HERMAN MELVILLE

Tackling tense can't be that hard, right? Well, the choice is not so much about being a hard one as it is about using a tense correctly and consistently. We've written earlier about just letting the story flow out of you and getting it all down on the page. You can always go back and clean things up. But, at the same time, beware that you maintain the correct tense. We provide this caution because, in our day-to-day lives, we often switch tense cavalierly in speech and don't even realize we are doing it. Yet when we read those same words, the change stands out and detracts rather than endearing your reader to the story.

Another caveat: it's not that you can't switch, but once again, know why you did. Be sure it's a purposeful move. If you use this as a sort of fine-bristled paint brush to effect emotion in your readers from your art piece, that is good. If you do it with a broad-bristled brush, it will only mar your masterpiece. Two examples:

> Example 1: John stood and stared. He couldn't believe his eyes. The body before him lay still, unmoving. *Is he dead?* John runs to get help, or starts to, but then turns and initiates CPR on his best friend in the world.

> Did you notice the tense change? It's jarring, isn't it? It's not that the scene isn't expected, but your mind is expecting different words. Let's look at a second attempt.

> Example 2: John stood and stared. He couldn't believe his eyes. The body before him lay still, unmoving. *Is he dead?* John asked himself. In his mind, he saw himself running to get help, but in truth he knew there was no time for that. He knelt and quickly moved to perform CPR on his best friend.

Here, a change in tense is enacted, but only to give insight into John's immediate thought (thought is almost always going to be in present tense), but with a little more finesse, and with purpose. The first example used the wide-bristled brush and marred the scene and the effect we wanted to make. In the second example, we used the fine-bristled brush to add a little subtle color and emotion to the scene. We put the present tense to indicate his thought as it occurs in real time. His thought is also placed in italics to indicate this, and we remain with his thoughts for one more sentence. That following sentence is not his direct thought (the actual thought inside his head), however, so it does not go in italics. The text then turns back to past tense as that is the tense of the overarching story.

This example illustrates another point: keep the overarching tense of your story consistent. This will provide consistency for your reader. As shown above, the change in tense is to add to your art, not detract from it.

There are only three tenses from which you can choose: past, present, future. The prevalence of their use in writing is also in that order from most used to least used. Allow us to address them in reverse order so we can move toward spending the most time on the most used of the three.

Future Tense. While using this tense is technically feasible, we're not sure anyone has ever done a complete novel in this way. Why? It's extremely hard to do while keeping your readers engaged. Reason? Your entire novel would be about what is going to happen and never about what is *actually* happening. That's rather strange—and likely the way readers will see it. How do you keep their interest in such a piece of writing? We may be proven wrong, but don't think you can.

We're not saying you can never use future tense, but we think it would have to be used in a limited fashion for a specific purpose. Think of the fine-bristled brush technique we just talked about—use it subtly but with great purpose.

To be honest, the only thing that directly comes to mind would be that of a fortune-teller or prophet of some kind. Yet that could be the drama and catalyst needed to make your story unique or head in a totally different direction. It could be used to propel your protagonist in a new direction, be the reveal of something deeply hidden in their psyche or past, or make him or her do something they would never have done otherwise.

Or it could reveal an ominous future that will keep the reader looking for clues that support the future prophecy.

One example I (Randy) can give is from my book *Promised Kingdom*. A prophet tells Elsbeth, one of the story's main characters, she will become a doorway, someone others will seek to emulate. Elsbeth becomes quite puzzled by this statement, but it serves to push the reader toward becoming more engaged to find out what the ominous prophecy really means and how it will be revealed. So this is a *limited* use of future tense.

Present Tense. Writing in present tense is not something new, but it is exceedingly difficult to do well. As with everything, there are pros and cons in using this technique. Again, be purposeful in how you use it.

Using present tense can make your writing more "movie-like." It will read somewhat like you envision a movie would unfold. While that may be true, as a writer you are more limited in how you can reveal a scene to your reader. Everything is from one person's point of view. Movie producers can switch cameras from one character to another and keep the audience from becoming confused because the audience has visual cues as to which character they are focused on. This is more difficult in a novel. You can't just switch without giving the reader a cue that you have switched to another character whose viewpoint you are now referencing. But moving your reader to a point of confusion is not what you want; she is likely to not read on, and that is a bad—very bad—outcome. Switching characters can be done, but it must be purposeful and done with great care. Some authors only change at the beginning of a new chapter and, even then, state which character's viewpoint the chapter is speaking from. (*The Killer Angels*, by Michael Shaara, on the three-day Battle of Gettysburg in 1863, and the *Incense Road* trilogy, by Tracy Higley, are two fantastic examples of this done well.) However you do it, the switch must appear natural and be easy for your readers to understand.

This technique also allows you to get your readers remarkably close to your character and understand the character's perspective and how they think. (You experience this in amazing, rich ways in *The Killer Angels*.) This can be extremely appealing to a reader. Yet it is difficult to maintain this over the course of an entire novel as the reader is living in the here and now with the character, and present tense can't skip across long time periods easily.

An important thing to mention is to not confuse present tense with active voice. Active voice can be in any tense. Just because you write something in present tense does not necessarily make it active voice. Here are some simple examples:

Active: Present Tense: The monkeys like the bananas you gave them.

Active: Past Tense: The monkeys liked the bananas you gave them.

Active: Future Tense: The monkeys will like the bananas you give them.

Passive: Present Tense: The bananas you gave are liked by the monkeys. (It's not hard to see how awkwardly that sentence reads.)

Passive: Past Tense: The bananas you gave were liked by the monkeys.

Passive: Future Tense: The bananas you give will be liked by the monkeys.

Active means the action of the verb is conducted by the subject of the sentence. Passive means the verb is taking action on the subject of the sentence. In the first three sentences, the monkeys are doing the liking no matter if in present, past, or future tense. In the second three sentences, the bananas are being liked, but bananas themselves are inert, so it's pretty poor writing. (Almost all the time. There could be a stylistic reason— rare, though, overall—to construct a sentence in this manner.)

Past Tense. This is probably the most common of the three tenses used in writing. Not only is it easier, it is also more easily understood—and expected—by most readers. And yet, this tense still has a great deal of versatility. First, you could say that, because it has become the expected, it is almost invisible to the reader. That is, past tense is the least jarring to a reader. Any tense, potentially, can become invisible to the reader (future tense might be an exception), but past tense is the one most likely to be invisible from the start and least jarring to a reader.

Past tense is also the most flexible of the three tenses. Even through past tense, the reader can feel as though things are happening in the present. This allows the reader to skip through time more easily than one can in present tense without things sounding weird. One also has the capability of showing the points of view of more characters (see chapter *P: Point of View*). This is likely why many readers enjoy reading novels written in past tense more than any other tense.

Let's conclude the discussion on past tense by again saying to be purposeful in the tense you use. Also, use any change in tense for effect or to elicit a specific emotion in your reader. But keep the overarching tense constant throughout your writing.

Before we close this chapter, we should discuss a few nuances to tense: type and mood.[12, 13]

Again, the three types of **tenses**:

1. Present

2. Past

3. Future

Each **type** of tense may be:

1. simple (conveying present action)

2. perfect (conveying a past or future action)

3. continuous (conveys what is happening right now)

4. perfect continuous (conveys what has happened in the past and is still happening)

The **moods** of each type of tense show what is possible, or hypothetical:

1. indicative (states, asks, or denies a fact)

2. subjunctive (contrary-to-fact and hypothetical statements)

3. imperative (requests and commands)

Short examples of each are helpful. We have a chart, but it covers a few pages, so we've placed it in Appendix B at the back of this book. Turn there to see the various uses of tense, type, and mood. A writer has many tools in her or his toolbox!

T * T * T * T * T * T * T

Tips and Information

From the Author

- The tense you choose should be consistent throughout your writing.
- Tense switching can sometimes be included if done with purpose for a particular reason.
- The most common tense used in writing is past tense.
- Telling a story is more difficult utilizing present tense and future tense than using past tense.

From the Editor

- The biggest point to reiterate: please don't—at random, or even in any case, without a clear (but infrequent) purpose—jump around in tenses in your work. It is maddening to the reader . . .
- . . . This, if done, simply shows the writer hasn't carefully read over, or taken care with, her or his work.
- Those things said, let's end this chapter with the good news: don't obsess with worry over this. It's important, but you'll get it! This is where reading back over your work is really going to come in. (Yes, begin writing with the idea that you will not be switching tenses.) The companion book, our guide to self-editing, will hit this more, talking about the importance of self-editing.

Chapter 21

U

Unnecessary Words

"You can always edit a bad page. You can't edit a blank page.
JODI PICOULT

Unfortunately, being humans who live on a verbose planet, we often speak words—even many words—that are unnecessary. We have come to accept that from our fellow human travelers. Much of this is due to bad habits that become engrained over the years. In many aspects we have come to accept the habits rather than consciously ridding ourselves of bad verbal faux pas.

People talk a lot when they are nervous (again, engrained in human nature), and listeners tend to put up with it. But you're a writer. Your job is to be disciplined. Always remember this: the reader is *reading* with a far more critical eye than they will ever *listen* critically to a speaker. Short exercise: give a close listen to any public speaker, particularly pastors and politicians. They will say things over and over, and the listener is forgiving because of the energy of the moment, the pedestal they have given the speaker in their minds, or both. But put those exact words in print, in a book, and they look poor, maybe even awful. So we must be disciplined.

When unneeded words are placed on paper, they stand out. Or they decrease the pizazz we're trying to provide our readers. If we have a word count quota, we don't want to meet that with words of inconsequence, but with words that impact and endear our readers to our work. Remember: do everything with purpose.

So, what are these word culprits? They fall into three main categories: *pleonasms, tautologies,* and *anaphora*. Let's look at each. (We're sorry these terms sound so boring and technical. It's just what they're called! But these are important pitfalls to avoid. If nothing else, these words might give you a new Scrabble word or two with which you can impress your friends the next time you play!)

Pleonasm

Pleonasm means using words that add no increase in meaning to a sentence. What does this mean? Well, writers often use filler words that contribute no added benefit to the reader. These are not bad words per se, but our colloquial speech has used them so routinely we unconsciously add them to our writing without really meaning to do so. Here are a few, with some examples.

That. What's wrong with *that*, you ask? Well, nothing. It has its proper place in spots but tends to creep into places it is not needed.

Mary realized that she was not getting Harry's attention, so she yelled louder.

See anything wrong there? It's definitely a sentence someone would say, but the word *that* in this sentence is totally inconsequential. It adds nothing and actually detracts from the sentence.

Mary realized she was not getting Harry's attention, so she yelled louder.

Sounds better, right? When you go through your draft, you'll be surprised at how many *thats* are in your manuscript. The number you find will likely be a good deal more than you realized. Check and see.

Now, of course, you won't need to delete every *that* in your writing. There are places it is needed.

Mary saw Jack had taken that specific manuscript.

In this sentence, *that* is needed because it is identifying which manuscript was taken. Also, the sentence doesn't make any sense if we remove the word *that*.

Here are some other words to carefully peruse your writing for; they simply may not be needed.

Really. Often, this word is superfluous. (It really is.) You can either remove it completely or look for a better word choice.

This apple pie is really great.

You can delete it altogether: *This apple pie is great.* The second sentence has the exact impact of the first one.

Likely, with the first sentence, you were trying to say it is better than great. A better word choice will convey that in a stronger way: *This apple pie is marvelous.* Or: *This apple pie is scrumptious.*

Very. Again, this word can be left out, or you can choose a better modifier.

I come to this restaurant very often.

This sentence reads with the same intent—and even better— by deleting the modifier.

I come to this restaurant often.

Or you can choose a stronger modifier: *I come to this restaurant quite often.*

Or perhaps make a better word choice: *I come to this restaurant frequently.*

Want another way to remember this? I (Bob) truly dislike the use of this word in nearly all uses. I equate it, in my mind, with the word *vanilla* (very = vanilla). Now, I can enjoy a good vanilla ice cream like anyone else, but we all know what the word, in an overall sense, means (and why Ben & Jerry's, percentage-wise, doesn't sell much vanilla). To use the word very as an adjective is . . . vanilla. Very much so. Almost all the time, just skip it.

Just. This is similar to very. Most of the time this word can be left out completely without changing the meaning of your sentence.

Jill just stood there without expression.

Jill stood there without expression.

Now, we can't say there is absolutely no difference between the two sentences. The difference is subtle. The first sentence tends to imply Jill being more motionless than does the second. Yet many times this subtlety is not needed. Sometimes it may be. We suggest you use the word judiciously so the subtlety comes though when needed. If used too often, the subtleness gets lost on your readers.

Leading words and phrases. This would include these choices: *so, mostly, most times, often, oftentimes, in order to, as you can see.*

In order to see the bird in the tree, stand here.

To see the bird in the tree, stand here.

The difference is clear. The words "in order" in the first sentence do absolutely nothing but take up space.

Still better, rearrange the clause to have no leading phrase:

Stand here to see the bird in the tree.

The other words and phrases above: you can do similar exercises with them. Again, you don't have to avoid these words and phrases altogether, but use them judiciously and with purpose.

Adverbs in general. While there is nothing wrong with adverbs, they typically don't add much meaning.

The movie was truly marvelous.

Standing with your neighbor in the yard, go ahead and say that if you believe it. Your neighbor will smile and be glad for your movie review. But please, don't write this way. There's a clunkiness, a *thud*, a slow-down, a woodenness, that the reader doesn't need. (In reading it, can't you just hear the *thud*?)

The adverb should be simply deleted: *The movie was marvelous.* Marvelous is marvelous. Here's yet another hidden tip of strong writing: let the strength of the word speak for itself. Don't feel like you have to throw a necklace around the pig; it already looks like a pig without you working too hard to show it truly is a pig.

Yet one can see an adverb as useful if one character is expressing deep emotion to another. In such a case, the adverb may be appropriate since you are conveying a sincerity to your reader that goes beyond a simple understanding.

Mary reached and cupped Brian's cheek with her hand. "Brian, I'm truly sorry for what I said earlier." Her eyes moistened. "Can you forgive me?"

While the word *truly* can be left out, adding it here elevates Mary's apology. The other legitimate thing about this use is it is being said in dialogue, so Mary, yes, might have spoken just this way to Brian.

If adverbs are overused in these cases, however, the subtlety of using them gets erased from your reader's perspective.

Forms of to be: *am, is, are, was, were, being, been.* See if something more active and less passive can be used:

Tom is being jealous of John.

Not so good. Why not say: *Tom is jealous of John.*

Adam was thinking hard for a solution.

Not so good. Why not say: *Adam thought hard for a solution.*

Sometimes this can be as simple as omitting the form of *to be*, and at other times replacing the passive form with an active form. This will not always be possible, but consider active voice whenever you can.

Two or more words used together but conveying no additional information. There are numerous examples of these, so a few short examples should suffice.

Jane said she saw the UFO with her own two eyes.

If Jane saw it, then it had to be with her eyes, and like the vast majority of humans, she has two of them.

Craig packed his parka. He would need it when they explored the Alaskan frozen tundra.

The definition of tundra is that it is a frozen landscape.

Jennifer raised up the lid of the pot on the stove.

The word *raised* implies the upward movement; *up* is monumentally unnecessary.

We could go on, but you get the point. Trust us, these sneak up on you, on all of us as writers, more than you think. Look at your sentences and see what is not needed. Be sure each sentence is as powerful as it can be. And remember, there are exceptions to all cases. Just know you have made the exception and for what reason. Be judicious. Read your sentences carefully.

Tautology

Tautology means repeating words or phrases in a different way and thus giving the same meaning, a second time, to what has already been said. This is most often used in poetry and, unfortunately, has bled into other writing styles. While this can be used cleverly in writing, make sure it is with clear intent.

Sally laughed and waved her hand in a dismissive gesture. "Oh, Henry is always making such predictions about the future."

Predictions are always about the future, so the prediction couldn't be about anything else. The second sentence would be much better as:

"Oh, Henry is always making such predictions."

Sometimes, things may not be quite as obvious.

Jane committed the unforgiveable faux pas and picked up her dinner fork rather than her salad fork.

Not a bad sentence, but picking up the dinner fork is the faux pas. Perhaps something like this would be better:

Jane picked up her dinner fork rather than her salad fork. Her fiancé cringed as he shook his head slightly while watching her. He knew this faux pas would be held against her.

The second version conveys the seriousness of Jane's actions and her mistake—at least to her fiancé's family. The second version takes more words (nearly twice as many, in fact), but tells the story much better.

Using a tautology is not always wrong. One can be used to drive home a point, add whimsy, or provide the traits of a character.

"I saw the grizzly, a very big bear," Pepper said, eyes growing wide. Jill laughed, causing Pepper to give her a confused look.

John rolled his eyes. Pepper always said such ignorant things, *he thought.*

This purposeful use of a tautology from Pepper allows the writer to tell the reader something about all three characters.

Go through your writing and delete tautologies when they are not used with a clear purpose, or at least see how they can be used—but only with direct intent.

Anaphora

Anaphora means the repeating of words or phrases in consecutive sentences. Again, this could be on purpose or, more typically, unintentional. For example:

John ran toward the hangar. He got there just in time to see the two-engine jet pull forward. He ran after it waving his hands to get the pilot's attention. He ran with all his might to stay with the plane. He ran out of energy, and the distance between him and the plane grew wider. He watched it take off and dropped his head. How would he ever get home now for the birth of his son?

We can see how the word *he* is used repeatedly at the beginning of each sentence. This makes the paragraph seem monotonous even when the action is not. In such cases you need to reword the sentences or rearrange words within certain sentences so the reader can stay focused on the action and not get lost on the sentence structure. Try this:

John ran toward the hangar. He hoped he was in time to catch the two-engine jet, his only hope of getting home in time for the birth of his son. Yet the plane was pulling out of the hanger as he approached. Waving his hands furiously, he tried to get the pilot's attention. To his horror, the plane passed him by. He ran after the plane with all his might, but his energy drained quickly and the distance between him and the plane grew wider. With despair, John dropped his head as the plane took off. How would he ever get home now?

There are times, though, when you want a use repeated for a particular purpose.

The more Stephen thought about his conversation with his professor, the angrier he became. After all, he was the one who wrote almost the entire document. He came up with the idea for the project. He had set up the discussion meetings. He had done all the research. He wrote the first rough draft. John wrote a five-sentence introduction, and the professor gave a higher grade to John. It wasn't fair in the least, Stephen thought.

In this case, the repeated word *he* for multiple sequential sentences is used to drive home a point. So, while redundant, its repeated use has a purpose: to emphasize to the reader all the work Stephen had done on the document. This helps the reader understand Stephen's anger with his professor.

There are other words and phrases you should be aware of. They don't fit into these three categories, as you can't just delete the word and have the sentence still make sense. As writers, we need to replace these words and phrases with other words and phrases that are more descriptive of what we truly want to convey. Again, these are not absolute requirements. Just remember to ask yourself if what you have is the best word or phrase for what you want to convey.

Other Suggestions

Three other suggestions to consider when possible:
(1) Use action verbs when possible:

The family is having dinner.

The more nondescriptive use of *having* in this sentence can be changed to something more meaningful, such as the following:

The family is enjoying dinner.

(2) Limit use of adjectives: use adjectives when they are important for the reader.

Amber wore a red dress to the festive party and ate too many salty nachos with zesty queso dip.

Which of these adjectives are actually necessary? That depends upon what is happening. Remember when we talked about broad-stroke brushes and fine-stroke brushes? Use adjectives like a fine brush to add enhancement to what you convey. (As an exercise, try writing this sentence a little better, a little tighter. Hint: parties are usually festive by nature; nachos are naturally salty.)

(3) Avoid clichés when possible.

If you do use them, use sparingly. They are like salt. A little goes a long way. There are times you can use them more often, but not generally. For example, in my (Randy) science fiction series The Erabon Prophecy trilogy, Nuke the astronaut was always using Earth clichés, and his alien friends had no idea what he was talking about. This added a bit of whimsy to the story, enhanced the fact he was the actual alien in the world he was living in, and helped define the character's personality. As we have said with everything else, write with purpose. (From Bob: I edited these books. I can tell you Nuke's cliché-riddled speech worked well, but only because it was done with a clear purpose!)

Refer to Appendix C for more suggestions on this chapter's topic.[14, 15] We think if you take the content and context of this chapter to heart, you'll enhance your masterpiece, and your readers will appreciate the extra effort. Realize your readers will not know the time it took you to do this, but they will appreciate the elegance of your work.

At the bottom is the irony: they will appreciate what they don't realize you have done. But they will notice if you don't take the time to do it.

U * U * U * U * U * U * U

Tips and Information

From the Author

- **Useful, quick tip:** use the Find feature in Microsoft Word (or whichever word processor you use) to search for unnecessary words that should be eliminated.
- **Unless you are purposefully** starting successive sentences with the same word to create a certain mood in your writing, this is a habit best avoided.

- Utilize different words or phrases that may mean the same as has already been stated so your writing does not become repetitive.
- Use action words when possible, and use adjectives and adverbs sparingly for maximal effect.

From the Editor

- Utilize the strength of words and phrases, allowing them to speak for themselves. Often, using extra words to try to bulk up one's writing isn't the best of ideas.

- Unnecessary words should be excised from your writing (in many to most cases). Words like: *that, really, very,* and *just*. (They are usually just really, very bad. Very vanilla.)

- Universally, this has been studied and written about many times and in many ways: the reader of our time has a shorter attention span than any Homo sapiens in the history of our planet. People are more distracted than ever. This is not news. You have the same twenty-nine devices they do. So you *must* keep them engaged with your writing. Clunky words have the opposite effect.

Chapter 22

Vary Your Lengths: Sentences, Paragraphs, Chapters

"Start writing, no matter what. The water does not flow until the faucet is turned on."
Louis L'Amour

Variety is the spice of life, as they say. This chapter's thought has already been in your toolbox. Or, perhaps not. But even if you had this somewhere in the back of your mind, maybe you haven't thought so consciously of it while writing or when going back over your writing. So we think it's worth devoting an entire chapter to the topic. This is one of those things that is so simple and yet does so much for the reader.

First, a quick word of caution. It is good to vary how you say things, but remember to remain in character with your character, if you will. If it is something the character would not say or do, then even though the word, phrase, or expression is different, it could prove jarring to your readers. As always, do everything with purpose.

Now to the main point: if not given variety, sentence structure can become wooden, dull, repetitive. Though a different way to look at this, consider many movies. After all, your writing is running like a movie in your reader's mind, right? Good filmmakers know to vary the lengths of scenes. Some scenes are emotional and filled with drama or poignancy and need time to play out. Other scenes are quick, punchy, filled with action or some other simple element that doesn't need much time. The variance in elements keeps the movie fan watching, glued to the scenes before them.

There are so many movies that demonstrate this point well that to mention just one or two seems wrong. But let's take one anyway: an old (for Bob) favorite (if the early '90s is considered old, and I guess it is) is *Last of the Mohicans*, the James Fenimore Cooper classic brought to life. The movie opens with a continual-action hunting scene, but there are long dialogue scenes, intense war scenes, a love scene that moves, not slowly as you would expect but quickly (which of itself is a sort of surprise), and there are two scenes in which a marching army is ambushed by Native American warriors from the surrounding woods. While the latter scenes move quickly to heart-pounding action, they are preceded by slow, still marching in which the anticipation builds like water rising in a dam. As the battalions move along slowly, with only the clinking of metal, and everything else still, one can *feel* the ambush in each scene about to launch—just like the moment the water will breach a dam. The movie is a great example of varying the lengths of scenes, and with great purposes.

Now back to your writing. Why can't you do the same? You can!

First, let's talk about sentences. Vary their length, how you structure them, and how you provide dialogue tags. An example is given here; see how this short scene impacts you.

> *Sam decided to go to the market. Her cupboards were almost bare. Sam knew she had to go today. Otherwise, she had no idea when she would get there. Yet her car was with the mechanic, so she needed to get her neighbor Edna to take her. She picked up the phone, dialed, and waited for Edna to answer.*
>
> *"Hi, Edna. This is Sam."*
>
> *"Oh, hi Sam. Everything okay?" Edna asked.*
>
> *"Oh, all's fine. Just wondering if you're doing your grocery shopping today?" Sam asked in return.*
>
> *"I was just about to head out the door. Why? Need anything?" Edna asked.*
>
> *"Oh, can I go with you?" Sam paused. Not hearing a response from Edna, she continued. "My car is in the shop, and I really need to get groceries today. I promise to be done by the time you are."*
>
> *After another pause, Edna responded. "Oh, sure. It'll be fun to catch up on the way."*
>
> *"Thanks, Edna. I'll be right over."*

Not the most riveting writing, we grant you. Did you notice the clear issues? There isn't much variation in sentence structure, the word *oh* is used too many times, and the dialogue tags are always in the same place. It's quite wooden (there's that word again). It's dull, repetitive, boring.

Now let's see if by changing some elements the writing can become more engaging.

Sam closed the cupboard door and groaned. She realized she needed to get groceries, but her car was still with her mechanic. What do I do? *she asked herself. This was the only day she had to accomplish this chore. An idea hit her. Edna. She picked up the phone and punched in her neighbor's number.*

As soon as Edna answered, Sam dove in. "Hi, Edna, forgive my intrusion. But will you be going to the grocery today?"

Edna gave a small chuckle. "Well, your timing is impeccable. I was just about to head out the door. Need anything?"

"May I go to the store with you?" *Sam asked. She knew she sounded more desperate than she intended, and Edna likely thought this an imposition, but she had to get groceries today.* "I'm sorry, my car is in the shop, and I really need to get this done. I promise not to be an inconvenience to you."

After a long pause, Edna responded. "Oh, sure. It'll be fun to catch up on the way."

On the inside, Sam breathed a sigh of relief. "Thanks, Edna. I'll be right over."

You'd probably agree that the sentence lengths, dialogue attributions, and sentence structure are more varied in the second example. While it still doesn't make for the most exciting scene ever, to say the least, it does make it more interesting than the first example. So take this to heart. Variety, as we stated in the opening line to this chapter, is the spice of life. That remains true for your writing and your readers' enjoyment as well.

As you have longer sections without dialogue and just action, or backstory, do the same thing with **paragraphs**. Shorter paragraphs interspersed among longer ones keep the reader visually alert, interested, stimulated.

Last, do the same with **chapters**. Ever read a book with, say, five forty-page, monolithic-feeling chapters? You know the overall effect on that book's reader. It takes a fantastically engaging writer, or material, to keep readers plugged in.

A few side points as we move to closing this chapter.

A tip: repetitions and redundant sentence structures are more easily discovered when you read them aloud. That does take more time, but the number of these types of errors will be more easily caught. There are several ways to do this. First, you can have someone else read your draft and make comments. This is a little tricky because if they know you well, they may not tell you all your errors as they want to be kind. But this is not a time for kindness, so while we wouldn't say not to let your friends read your drafts, don't let that be the only way you try to identify such writing issues. Second, read it aloud yourself. While this is probably not what you want to do, you will be glad you did. And third, if reading that long gets tiring, most word processors, and several apps, now do that for you. While you won't get all the inflections in your work, it will help you find most of the shortcomings, and that is what you are trying to find. Give these a try. You won't regret it.

* * * * *

Vain Words and Phrases: Avoid Them

Vain words are a bit similar to *U: Unnecessary Words*, but we think there is a difference between these two types of words even though they may be similar in nature. While certain words and phrases are necessary, if we use them repeatedly, they become vain words and don't elicit the effect on our readers we truly want.

This was mentioned to some extent in *S: Show Don't Tell*. Be sure you have multiple ways to express similar emotions. Although you are being repetitive in emotions, you are not being repetitive in word choice, and this helps these expressions not become vain repetitions to your readers.

Too many writers write to try to impress with big words. If you want a solid, even sneaky, tip that will endear you to your reader, use a simpler word over a more complex, or convoluted, one every time. To write with too many of those proverbial sixty-four-dollar words becomes quite the vituperative experience for the reader. It's also an insulting one. (Now, which of the last two sentences did you grasp better, more intuitively?)

There's a fun phrase that I (Bob) share with some golfing buddies. (It's pretty much rehearsed by this point.) When someone hits a towering, impressive shot, one of the group members invariably says, "Wow, that had quite the apex." To which another in the group will reply: "It was really high, too." Hopefully you are soaking in—or even just getting—the point.

A final note: this rule of using simpler words over complex ones will serve you about 99 percent of the time, so use it. But yes, as we've said throughout, there are exceptions. The rare, complicated word that is the only word that can be used to mean what it says is the one to use when no other words can express the same idea. Recently, I (Bob) edited a writer's memoir in which he used the word *apophasis*. (Look that one up for fun if you don't know it.) In this instance, that word was left in his text because it takes many words to say what apophasis does—but also because, stylistically, the word actually did work with the mystical type of scene the author was setting. However, it's a fairly rare word. So you have to be careful when you break the rules. And sometimes, a shiny word can provide a strong pacing or smile to the reader—but only if they grasp the word easily enough, or at least don't have to run to an online dictionary too many times.

V * V * V * V * V * V * V

Tips and Information

From the Author

- **V**acillate sentence structure between long and short sentences to help the flow of your story.

- **V**ariability should be used in your descriptions. Be careful not to use the same words or phrases repeatedly through your story.

- **V**oluminous backstory should be treated carefully. Limit it or weave it throughout your overall story.

- **V**alue the use of Microsoft Word's read-out-loud feature or other methods to hear your story aloud; that will catch many errors as you hear them.

From the Editor

- Vary the lengths of your sentences, paragraphs, and chapters. It's a gift to the reader. It's one tool—but a strong one—to help them stay engaged.
- View the writing of other writers to see how they do this. Watch excellently paced movies. (A caution: I have read well-known authors who write in monolithic paragraphs. Often, these kinds of books are ones with a more academic bent. Simply, they can get away with it because of their platform, the material, or both. Most of us don't have their platform.)
- Very rarely, when making a choice between an impressive sounding, complicated word and one that is simpler and yet instantly makes the point, should you choose the first. (There can be rare exceptions for well-thought-out reasons.) Most of the time, use the simpler word. It serves the reader better.

Chapter 23

Ways of Writing

"And by the way, everything in life is writable about if you have the outgoing guts to do it, and the imagination to improvise. The worst enemy to creativity is self-doubt."
SYLVIA PLATH

Writing a novel can be accomplished in two main ways: being a "plotter" (a writer who plans everything out) or creating as a "pantser" (writing by "the seat of one's pants," also meaning the story morphs as one writes).

A "plotter" maps out all aspects of her or his novel (overall story plot, characters, character personalities, subplots, crises, resolutions, and end of story) before they put one word to the page. Granted, some will do this partially, or do internal mapping along the way. But most detail is thought out before it goes to the page.

A "pantser" just starts writing and lets things develop as the story unfolds. While pantsers may have a general idea of how the story will go, it nonetheless keeps morphing as it unfolds, and the writer simply yields to the flow.

Plotters make the story wield to their plans; pantsers let the story unfold naturally, and they go along for the ride.

Now the purpose of this chapter is not to tell you how to be a plotter or a pantser, and it definitely is not to tell you which one to be! It is to let you know of these broad approaches and then allow you to further explore what is most suited to your personality and writing style. Both are appropriate and acceptable. Neither is right; neither is wrong.

Here are some famous plotters.[16]

John Grisham, author of *A Time to Kill, The Firm, The Rainmaker, The Reckoning,* and dozens of others, says, "The more time I spend on the outline the easier the book is to write. And if I cheat on the outline, I get in trouble with the book."

J.K. Rowling, author of the *Harry Potter* book series, says she likes to do a basic, but detailed, outline and then fill in as she goes.

E.L. Stein, author of the *Goosebumps* books, says, "If you do enough planning before you start to write, there's no way you can have writer's block. I do a complete chapter-by-chapter outline."

Some famous pantsers:[17]

Margaret Atwood, author of the acclaimed *The Handmaid's Tale,* says, "... an image, scene, or voice ... I couldn't write the other way round with structure first. It would be too much like paint-by-numbers."

Pierce Brown, author of the *New York Times* bestselling book series *Red Rising*, says, "I sit down at my computer every day praying for a lightning strike."

Stephen King, also a *New York Times* bestselling author for such books as *Carrie, The Shining, IT, Shawshank Redemption*, and many, many others (and we've referred to his book on writing in this book), says, "Outlines are the last resource of bad fiction writers who wish to God they were writing masters' theses."[18] Ouch. That's pretty direct. As acclaimed as King is, we bet the three authors above who are plotters wouldn't agree.

A general comment, and let's take one from each camp: if you read some of King's writing memoir, you'll see he is huge on this point, almost disdainful of writing the other way. He uses the metaphor that writing as a pantser is almost like unearthing rare fossils. You write, you think, you dig. You keep unearthing the next move in the story as it is revealed to you, the creator, in the process.[19] It's quite interesting to at least consider this approach. But take Stein's point above: makes a lot of sense, no? It's a strong argument. If you've plotted well enough, the story will keep flowing. Now whether that's best for you, or not, is the question.

So, as you can see, no matter which side of the fence you land on, you're in good company. So don't worry about which you are, just understand which you are and go with it. But also know that you may have to develop a thick skin around the topic. As some of the quotes above show, some authors are adamant about their chosen approach. You must know which of the two you are and stick with it. Again: know yourself. If you are happy and comfortable with one of the two, that's all that matters.

And yes, there are grades in between, as Rowling, above, shows. Although cliché: you do you.

If you find yourself a plotter, you may like Amy Deardon's book, *The Story Template*, as we mentioned in *K: Keep Plots Identifiable* and *N: Number of Characters*. She has broken good writing down to a science. Check out her book if this is the side of the fence you feel comfortable on. Another resource if you are a plotter is Roy Peter Clark's *Writing Tools*. It can give you great ideas of how to plan your work effectively.

As far as we know, there are no good books on how to be a pantser. (Though you can learn much more about it in King's writing memoir.) After all, that's the whole idea, right? There are no formulae, just gut instinct, imagination, determination, and a vision of the beginning and end. The in-between is all about where your mind takes you.

If you don't know which you are, it's okay to explore both. Just start writing. Find out if you need to set the keyboard aside and begin to plot an outline before your mind will allow you to go on, or if you are thrilled just pecking away and letting the tide take you where it does.

It goes without saying, but allow us to say it: there are still many things you need to be careful about if you are a pantser. You may be creating characters along the way that you won't come back to until later, or for some time. You must keep the details consistent. For example, don't make the reader come back to a manipulative dad you introduced eight chapters ago to find he now has five children when he had three before (unless time, and natural reasons, clearly account for the addition).

You may wish to explore both of these approaches. You should be able to find out which you are and feel more confident in your choice.

Or you may find you're somewhat like Rowling who, in our view, is the closest to a hybrid of the authors we listed above.

* * * * *

There is one more thing to convey about ways of writing. What about time of day, and length of writing sessions? What's best in those two areas? We're certain if you were able to survey five hundred of the top active authors in the U.S., you'd probably get five hundred different daily writing plans. You simply must use what works for you.

Some are morning people, some mid-morning, some afternoons, and so on. We wouldn't recommend beginning your writing day late at night, but for some, it may be necessary. I (Bob) once read of a pastor-author who got up every day at 3:30 a.m. to write daily from 4 to 7 a.m. during his writing season of the year. Most of us haven't even begun to get the cobwebs cleared by 5:30 or 6, let alone be writing in strong form by that time, but hey, you do what works for you. And remember, an author as famous as Stephen King makes *reading* a large part of his day, setting aside the writing entirely for that portion of his schedule.

Length of time in a single writing session? Again, there is no formula that must be embraced. We'd probably recommend you stay at it for longer than ten minutes, and some people may need five- or ten-minute breaks every half-hour or so. Others can crank hard for three hours without so much as budging from the keyboard. (Strong bladders among those types!)

Number of newly created words per writing day or week? Again, this is entirely what works for you. You'd be amazed what just a little consistency can net you. I (Bob) once listened to a young adult author who was prolific, with dozens of titles to his name, say his daily goal was merely a thousand words. If you just write straight—even if it's not your best—you'll be surprised how quickly you can get to one thousand. Now, the goal isn't to write badly! Maybe just three hundred, four hundred, or five hundred words per day (with at least two to four hours at the keyboard; say, a third- to a half-day of writing, because you probably have a full-time job). Any of those goals may be a great and successful day for you. If you're a new writer and want to celebrate one hundred or 150 new words per day to which you have given some strong thought, that's great!

We have one final encouragement: do have a goal! In life, do we always hit our goals? Of course not. They are just that. But to have a daily goal of, say, five hundred words is better than having no idea how much you intend on any particular day.

W * W * W * W * W * W * W

Tips and Information

From the Author

- **W**riting style is typically one of two: planner or pantser. Yet you can also choose a combination of the two (the famous J.K. Rowling is a bit of a planner but also has strong leanings toward the latter). Just be true to yourself.

- **W**hether you are one type versus the other doesn't matter. Many great authors are one or the other. (See our examples in this chapter.)

- What will help your learning if you are a planner? There are several books on how to improve your planning process.

- While there are no books on how to be a better pantser, the very approach means you have free reign on how you work. That is the whole purpose of the approach: no formal planning process.

From the Editor

- Who you best are, planner or pantser, may be a journey in and of itself. Randy has great tips just above.

- Write nearly every day (plan break days, certainly) or at least a certain number of hours per week. Find what works for you. Seek to be consistent. A five-hour day one day and then not coming back for two weeks won't greatly help your craft. Seek more consistent, if shorter, efforts on a daily or (if you're working a full-time job or other jobs, which you are probably are) several-days-a-week basis.

- Words per day to write? Find a reasonable goal. But do make it reasonable. And do set a goal. Then find a day or week or writing season in which you have more time and can stretch yourself to longer goals.

Chapter 24

X-ing Out Favorite Texts

"When your story is ready for rewrite, cut it to the bone. Get rid of every ounce of excess fat. This is going to hurt; revising a story down to the bare essentials is always a little like murdering children, but it must be done."
STEPHEN KING

Xanadu is an idyllic place that doesn't exist, and that is true about your writing as well. Your writing will never be perfect even though you strive to reach that state. What does exist is hard work. There's a point when grit must be involved to get to your final draft. You may not feel like writing, or perhaps nothing good has come to you all week. (The overused term "writer's block" is often used to characterize this phenomenon.) But keep pushing. As an analogy, I (Bob, a bit of an amateur runner) have run on days when it was -8 degrees Fahrenheit and -20 wind chill, and in snow, solid rain, and patchy ice (you do it really, really carefully). You name it.

You'll do the same with writing. You'll have those foggy, snowy days in your mind.

So it is helpful to set goals. So what's the right goal for you? Great question. This ties somewhat to the suggestions made in the previous chapter about writing goals; only you can answer the larger question of your overall writing goal. You will learn your pace. Only you can decide what works for you.

Grit also involves some other things we must talk about, and this is the theme of this chapter. The following has been said in many ways by many writing coaches, but I'll (Bob) say it the way I like best: *Edit thyself ruthlessly.* This sometimes involves crossing out some of your favorite texts. There are a whole lot of words you can—and should—throw overboard. Speaking of ruthless, the early chapters of Zinsser's book *On Writing Well* are a fantastic read on this point.

In no particular order, here are some basic rules of digging into your writing, with grit (or, rather, gritting your teeth) and a heavy finger on the strikeout function, to make it read in a more engaging way.

- Look at what you just said in fifty words. Now rewrite it saying the same thing in thirty-five. Try it. You can do it. You'd be surprised how much you can do it.

Example (52 words, and not written particularly well):

She moved toward the door slowly and reached for the handle, fumbling to find it. When she turned the handle, the door barely moved—but move it finally did. It creaked as it did so. She slowly opened it to find . . . the empty room she feared would be empty.

Rewrite (30 words):

Slowly making her way to the door, she fumbled with the handle and got the door moving—barely. Creaking while it opened, it revealed what she feared: an empty room.

Which does more to keep you reading: the 52-word version or the 30-word one? Which pace will keep you moving forward, the longer one or the tighter, shorter one?

- Say what you need to say, then realize you've said it. Editors see this often: endlessly saying the same thing. This can be a real trap for preachers and other public speakers who write, and it happens for a simple reason: they want to drive home a specific point. On the stage, talking to an audience, repetition is a great thing! (All the great masters teach by repetition.) It works on the stage or behind the podium or pulpit. But not nearly so much in print. When you read the same lines retold the same way or even a slightly different way for a fourth time, you're saying to yourself that either the author is trying to meet a word quota, doesn't have new things to say, isn't working that hard to come up with new material, or some combination of the above. Don't keep saying the same thing. If there is a reason to do so, be sure it is purposeful and presented to your readers in such a manner they know it was done with purpose. Summarizing: saying the same thing over and over works well, sometimes great, on stage. In *writing*, it does not.

- Sometimes, crossing out significant amounts of text is needed. As we mentioned before, your first draft is simply that: a rough draft. It may be in fairly good shape and just needs a bit of work (best-case scenario), or it may be somewhat of a jumbled mess. That's okay. The former will come with time, so don't give up. Or even if it doesn't come, messy can always be made orderly. It just takes a little elbow grease and time. Or, in this case, brain grease. (Bad imagery. But you get the picture.)

There will be times, however, when going from messy to brilliant will be painful. There are instances where you have text you love, but it no longer fits as well as you thought because the story took a different turn. Your heart is telling you that you must keep it, but your brain is telling you otherwise. Listen to your brain. Although sometimes hard, try to look at it from your readers' perspectives. They don't have the emotional investment you do. Plus, they will never know the mental struggle you went through to get to your final product. You may even have to walk away for a time—even a few days—to gain a better perspective. If you find your readers don't need that text, then you must cut it—no matter how painful it may be.

I (Randy) mentioned earlier that in my first novel I had a very long backstory I wanted to tell. My rationale was I wanted the reader to understand the future time period, how it was predicted, and how it would come about. I really enjoyed all that information. Yet I finally had to look at this from my readers' perspectives. Many of them wouldn't necessarily care about so much detail and why the backdrop of the story was the way it was portrayed in my writing. Granted, some information was needed, but not so much that it took many chapters to present it all. Therefore, I chopped—heavily. It hurt. It really did. (What did King call it? A bit like "murdering children"—those words did feel like they were my children.) With that decision were all the many, tedious hours I spent researching this futuristic era that many have predicted: why it was to occur, how it was to occur, what it meant for those who would be living at that time, and why they needed to understand it. All that was now gone. No one would ever know the countless hours I spent researching this era so I could present it. I had to realize that my readers are not necessarily interested in the why. They just want a good story. So I took it all out, or at least the majority of it. I left just enough for my readers to understand the context of the beginning of the book. Even then, I had to cut and disperse it into bite-size chunks to allow the flow of the story to keep the readers' interest yet supply the necessary information at each point for understanding.

There's a small piece that one of the most famous authors of all time, Agatha Christie, wrote about one of her best-known works (but not the best known). This particular novel is my (Bob's) favorite of hers, hands down: *And Then There Were None*. (Sometimes titled *Ten Little Indians*.) It's the psychological thriller of ten people being murdered one by one on an isolated island with only those ten on the island, and each person growing increasingly paranoid as the killings continue with no clue as to who the murderer is. If you've never read it, it's brilliance on the page. Anyway, in one version's preface Christie wrote that no one, ever, would know how hard she worked at that novel, or to what depths. Nor would she try to explain it because only she would know. Mad respect for those words—at least from this corner.[20]

You may find yourself having to cut or dole out information in other ways as your manuscript develops. It may not be backstory. It could be riveting dialogue, a chapter you put sweat and tears into, or an action scene you are proud of—but how the story turned makes that piece now not so important. Oh, it's definitely important to you. After all, it's your baby. It took you many sleepless nights thinking about the scene: how to put it together, how to make it flow just right, and all those writes and rewrites to produce just the right beat and emotion for the reader. But if it no longer fits, you must give it the axe.

Final, important thought: don't throw it away entirely. You can either parse it out in various chapters if that makes sense to the storyline, or you can keep it for another book. Randy's long backstory we mentioned earlier became the impetus for four additional books! While cutting all the text was painful at the time, it led to better things for Randy later. Do what is in the best interest of your readers. You'll be grateful you did. And so will they. You hurt and bleed so they can enjoy.

X * X * X * X * X * X * X

Tips and Information

From the Author

- **X**-ing out text you really love is sometimes necessary because that text no longer fits your story.
- **X** marks the spot, or the treasure, and in your writing that comes through making every effort to write consistently, even when you don't feel like it.
- **X**erothermic writing may be in your first draft. (That X word means hot and dry; not exactly an inviting environment. Okay, I stretched a bit for that X!) Tweaking is always needed after the first draft through, along with

significant editing to make your words bloom and come alive, and that's okay.

- **X**anadu (or nearly that, anyway, as we said at the start of this chapter) for your writing only comes through significant efforts in self-editing. If you have the plot ironed out, finessing it is just a matter of work and time.

From the Editor

- **X**-ing out text can hurt. Reread the Stephen King quote at the top of this chapter. I can't provide a better tip than that. Or a more blunt one. King famously pulls no punches.

- **X**enolithic (a fragment of a gem hidden inside a larger rock) writing may be what your first draft is about, but know that your eloquent final version is in there. Writing takes grit: elbow grease and brain grease. Determine your goals and then work at those goals at a reasonable pace until they are met.

- **X**anthochroic (one with a pale complexion; again, I'm stretching with the X's a bit to say, essentially: dull writing) may be another way to describe your first draft. To make it colorful and more interesting, reread your work to make sure you are not making the same points repeatedly. This works in public speaking, but not with the written word. (Sure, there are some times to say something a second time for significance, or to remake a point made a few chapters ago. But see these as the exception.)

Chapter 25

Yield to the Flow

"If I waited for perfection, I would never write a word."
MARGARET ATWOOD

You as the author dictate what you say and how you want to say it. Yield to that flow. Many authors I (Bob) work with have the simple desire to tell their story: stories of overcoming a loved one's death, of mentoring, of watching an ailing parent die, of surviving an abusive spouse. Some write fiction: a story of a homeless man with significant mental health issues, a story of a young archaeologist stumbling on dinosaur bones, a television executive who keeps stumbling his way into God's path. Or a great writer of science fiction with a Christian bent, like my coauthor for this book, Randy.

There are so many things, and ways, to write. You don't have to start with publishing a book. Write your thoughts on

Facebook. Blog if you'd like. I know people who write for their church's online articles. Submit an article for an online review. Yelp review restaurants or ice cream shacks if you'd like. Write an article of thoughts to share with friends. You have a voice, and there's something you want to say. In time, perhaps, there is a book in there as well.

But there is the point when reality smacks you in the face. You must start writing. This stage is decidedly not glamorous. Perhaps not even fun. I've known writers who write from 4 to 7 a.m.; that is their writing time of the day. This takes serious discipline. Nothing says your writing has to be in the morning. But find time, make the discipline, to write.

Danielle Steel is one of the best-selling novelists of all time. She's sold more than a half billion books in the United States alone. (Yes, billion with a *b*.) She's written about the process of forcing herself to write. "When I actually get something to work on, I sit and . . . type until I ache so badly I can't get up. After twelve or fourteen hours, you feel as if your whole body is going to break in half. Everything hurts. . . . I've had cramps so badly when I sat typing that I couldn't move my hands for a couple hours, but I usually keep sitting there and pushing through."[21]

You're probably not to that point, and neither am I (Bob), but don't feel badly. Few are. We provide her dedication as an example of the extreme. You may not be there, but you can sit and work at your writing for one hour. If you wish. If you make yourself.

But this is the point of reality. It's an old adage, but nothing great ever comes without work, right? So again, ask yourself: what do I want to write? Start there. Reality will set in, and you will push through it.

* * * * *

There is another level of yielding to the flow. Don't get so lost in the rules of writing everyone is throwing your way that you lose the perspective of what you are trying to write. We have said this many times, but we felt the entire idea of yielding to the flow is so important it deserved its own chapter.

This was the one thing that really tripped me (Randy) up in the beginning, so I don't want it to happen for you. (The following few paragraphs are from Randy's perspective.)

I was really trying to follow all the rules. The books and blogs I were reading, by prominent editors and writers whose degree was in journalism or other writing professions, spouted all sorts of advice. They would say such things as: *never ever do so and so; never use these words*; or *remember to always put a comma after a conjunction*. I took them all to heart and rewrote my book with all those rules only to find out that my book read worse and not better. I kept asking myself: *why?* I followed all the rules. *My writing should be stellar.* But it wasn't. Also, I began to see that following a certain "rule" would seem to contradict other "rules."

What I began to see and understand was that these writers, while trying to impart their wisdom and be helpful, were not being entirely truthful. These were not rules, per se, but guidelines that work most of the time—not all the time. Rather than saying *never use* or *never do,* they should have said *never overuse* or *never overdo.* My writing journey led me to understand that good grammar is not always good, and a rule becomes just a guideline. Why do I say this? Because it is all about your reader, not about the rules. Yes, you should definitely know the best writing guidelines, and even rules, because the majority of the time the rules are in fact best to be followed. Why? Because they lead to good writing. Yet the rules may not always elicit the emotion you want your readers to feel. So, know the rules, but then know why you broke one. For instance, know why you might have a comma here and yet no comma there. Know that, typically, a comma should go there, but you chose to leave it out—and know why you made that choice.

Let me provide a simple example. Let's follow the rules:

Jamie couldn't stand it any longer. She had to tell Sarah her helpful advice was not helpful at all. It was only irritating. Before she had time to compose herself, she saw Sarah approach. She knew this was not good. She reminded herself to be gentle. Yet Sarah started talking, and all inhibition went out the window.

"Sarah!" Jamie said. Her tone was much louder than she had intended.

Sarah stopped midsentence; her eyes grew wide. "Is something wrong?"

Jamie held up her hands. "I know you mean well, Sarah. But your advice is not helpful. It is not helpful at all. I just need you to stop with your so-called helpful advice. Do you understand?"

Sarah gave a slight nod. Her eyes began to water. "Well, if that is how you feel, I'll leave you alone."

Sarah walking off without speaking further caused Jamie to sigh. She now felt worse than ever.

Before we discuss this, let's look at a revision that doesn't follow all the rules:

Jamie couldn't stand it any longer. She had to tell Sarah her helpful advice was not helpful; it was irritating—extremely irritating. Before she had time to compose herself, she saw Sarah approach. This is not good, she thought. She reminded herself to be gentle. Yet when Sarah started talking, all inhibition went out the window.

"Sarah!" Jamie said, her tone much louder than intended.

Sarah stopped midsentence, her eyes wide. "Is something wrong?"

Jamie held up her hands. "I know you mean well, but your advice is not helpful—at all. Just stop it, will you? Just. Stop it! Do you understand?"

Sarah gave a slight nod as her eyes grew wet. "Well! If that is how you feel." She waited as if expecting an apology. Her cheeks turned a tinge of red. "Fine! I'll just leave then!"

Sarah stormed off without speaking further. Jamie sighed. She now felt worse than ever.

I think the main difference between the two is that by using less formal grammar, one can better portray the irritation Jamie is feeling. I was able to better transition her feeling to Sarah. In the first example, the formal manner didn't really allow Sarah to storm off, but to just leave. In the second example, we have some commas without conjunctions, and we have some one-word sentences. This allows the writer to create more drama. So we did not follow all the rules of grammar, but we did it with intent. It allows us to create a better emotional reveal to the reader.

* * * * *

While this example is rather simple, we hope it gives you the idea we're trying to convey. Break the rules, when needed, to create an experience for your reader. Yet know when you break the rules and why you did so. If you break the rules all the time, not knowing you did so, then you have nowhere to go to make a difference for your reader. (If someone shouts at you all the time, regardless of whether what they are saying is important, you won't really listen when they shout something that is important. It's the same here.) When you break the rules, your reader knows something is different, and this difference produces the impact you want.

Bottom line: be intentional. Everything you write should have purpose. Nothing should be merely filler. Your readers have invested their time and money in your story. Give them their money's worth. Make every sentence, every word, every punctuation intentional.

Y * Y * Y * Y * Y * Y * Y

Tips and Information

From the Author

- You should never get so lost in the rules of writing that you lose the creativity of your writing.
- Your creative process should shine, but know the rules, and also know why you did not follow a rule so you can support the rationale behind your decision.

- Yearn to be bias free, but understand that all writers and editors have biases. You do as well. Be aware of this fact.
- Yes, be intentional. Every word you write should have purpose.

From the Editor

- Yield to the story that's inside you, that you want to write. Tell yourself loudly that you have something to say, and work until you have told it.

- Yippee, you want to write. So ... write. It doesn't have to be a full book or novel. There are many outlets in which to write. Find one. Begin.

- You'll stay on your writing journey for a lifetime if you commit yourself to learning the craft of writing and yield to that journey. And that is encouraging news for any writer.

Chapter 26

Z

Zeal for Writing

"I must write it all out, at any cost. Writing is thinking. It is more than living, for it is being conscious of living."
ANNE MORROW LINDBERGH

Zeal to be a writer may not come naturally. Some people seem to exude it. For others, it's a huge struggle to pursue it. For still others, it seems just out of reach, even as much as they would like to have it. But wherever you are, sluggishness doesn't mean you can't get there. Let's start this final chapter with an analogy.

I (Bob) didn't start running with any level of seriousness until I was in my forties. Until then, I enjoyed other sports much more: tennis, pick-up basketball, golf. Running seemed boring; what was the point? Then one day I began to realize how healthy it was to move the body for at least a mile of constant motion. I'm not a fast runner. I won't set any records. But I do love to get out and simply run, to be alone with nature, my running pace, and my thoughts.

In the fall of 2019, a pastor friend told me about streak running. (No, not that. Not the thing from the seventies. With this streak running, all the clothes say on.) It's a challenge to run a minimum of one mile, every day, without fail—that is what creates the streak—no exceptions. (I always run outside, 365 days a year, but Streak Runners International accepts treadmill runs as well.)

On an early fall day, October 8, 2019, shortly after my mother's death (and somewhat because I wanted to do something to honor her), I decided to try it. It's interesting how a second straight day can turn to three . . . to nine . . . to twenty-three . . . to fifty-two with a Thanksgiving Day run . . . to day 365, day 731 (two years) . . . and so on. I always say there is only one way to meet such a goal: take the first step out the front door to the starting point at the end of your driveway and keep moving. Don't stop until you're at least 0.55 miles away before turning and coming back. (At a minimum. For my personal goal, I run at least 1.1 miles daily, just to be legalistic about it, and yet average more like 1.5 to two miles per day, doing longer runs on planned days.) As of the exact days we are editing back through this book, my streak is 1,509 consecutive days (a little more than four consecutive years).

You have to look at your writing the same way. It starts with your first 30-minute commitment in front of the keyboard (heck, do just 15 minutes if you want), and then you commit to writing every day. You won't hit it out of the park every day. You don't feel great when you run every day. There are days that are real slogs. It will be the same with your writing. But eventually you'll find you're on a writing streak—one month straight, never failing! Two months! Maybe you missed a few days, but you got to ten thousand words in a month and never thought you would. Look at you. You're getting somewhere.

Only you can tell the story you have to tell. One of my (Bob's) favorite books on writing is the William Zinsser classic *On Writing Well*. It's a relatively quick and simple read, and we highly recommend it. Zinsser writes about how difficult writing can be, but he emphasizes that only you can say what you have to say.

> "Who am I to say what I think?" [a writer] asks. "Or what I feel?"
>
> "Who are you not to say what you think?" I tell them. "There's only one you. Nobody else thinks or feels in exactly the same way."
>
> "But nobody cares about my opinions," they say. . . .
>
> "They'll care if you tell them something interesting," I say, "and tell them in words that come naturally."[22]

There is also much to say about not being pretentious, not putting on airs, not always reaching for the flowery or cheeky phrase just to make yourself sound intelligent (Zinsser's gem has plenty to say about this). Make your writing simple, strong, and to the point—and yet say *interesting* things—and your readers will love you.

And still, say things with confidence. Zinsser compares saying things without confidence to poor organizational leaders who waffle and can't say what they really should say. These are the types who . . .

"*don't inspire confidence—or deserve it*. The same thing is true of writers. *Sell yourself, and your subject will exert its own appeal. Believe in your own identity and your own opinions. Writing is an act of ego, and you might as well admit it. Use its energy to keep you going*"[23] *(emphasis ours).*

Another way to talk about zeal: *why* are you writing? Are you writing about what is important to you or what is important to your readers? Is there a difference? We think yes. It is somewhat like the phrase: all robins are birds but not all birds are robins. Readers who are passionate about what you are passionate about will find your work. Yet if you are not passionate about what your readers are passionate about, readers will likely be able to see through the façade. Passion—zeal—is an important aspect of writing. It's what gives that extra spark to make your writing stand out from others.

Your zeal for writing can be expressed in various ways. It could be simply the joy of writing. You love to use the right words, syntax, and punctuation to put just the right spin on a scene, conversation, or event. That will shine from your writing. It may be that you have a passion for a certain social, spiritual, or political position and you enjoy using stories to bring this to light. That will also shine from your writing. Maybe you have a passion for a certain genre and love to tell stories to your readers that elevate that genre. That too will shine through.

Still, we must say this: for your readers, your zeal is not enough. While your zeal is important to drive you and to seal your readers to your style of writing, your stories still must be written well. So get to the point that the zeal of writing can overlay your other zeal. That is when you endear your readers to you and your writing. They enjoy your writing not only because of your zeal for why you write but also from the way you write.

Both are important and require a devotion for them to be elevated enough for your readers to get involved and be enthralled in what they're reading.

If you don't already have it, develop a passion (a zeal) for writing. Develop a zeal for the why behind your writing, the way you write, and in how you communicate both. See Appendix D for more tips on how to motivate yourself in your writing career.[24] It is then your readers see the true you in your work, and they will want to read what you have to say. Isn't that the goal? Writer and reader becoming one in the zeal of the written word—the written word you have created. An endless world awaits you. Go for it!

Z * Z * Z * Z * Z * Z * Z

Tips and Information

From the Author

- **Z**eal for writing can be learned and developed.
- **Z**ero. That's what your writing is worth if you don't understand the why behind your writing. There is a why behind everything you do, so know the why.
- **Z**eal, however, by itself, is not enough for your readers; your writing must read well and resonate with the reader.

From the Editor

- **Z**en within the passion for writing may not come naturally, but like a runner on a daily running streak, you can develop it. (We use zen here as a synonym for peacefulness, a sort of self-peace with your writing.)

- **Z**insser's book *On Writing Well* contains key parts about self-motivation in writing. Read them if you can, particularly the part telling you to say what only you have the ability to say.

- **Z**ealous to write? Remember, start simple. Maybe it's just 30 minutes three days a week. Due to your work and other responsibilities, perhaps that is your reasonable limit. Hit it and celebrate! If and when you can do more, enjoy hitting those goals too.

Appendix A
Adjective Order in Lists
(from Chapter 3)

If multiple adjectives are listed within a sentence, this is the order of use recommended by the following websites:

- Straus, Jane, "Arranging Multiple Adjectives: The Blue Book of Grammar and Punction," Grammarbook.com, https://www.grammarbook.com/blog/commas/arranging-multiple-adjectives/ (accessed Aug. 1, 2023).

- Cambridge Dictionary, English Grammar Today, Order of adjectives, https://dictionary.cambridge.org/us/grammar/british-grammar/adjectives-order (accessed Aug. 1, 2023).

The table below provides the suggested order. Note: the right column simply provides examples.

1. quantity	*one, two, four*	7. color	*black, white, red*
2. opinion	*talented. pretty, boring*	8. pattern	*striped, spotted, checked*
3. size	*big, small, tall*	9. origin	*Swedish, African, Cuban*

4. condition or quality	lean, easy, cold	10. material	glass, wood, brick
5. shape	square, round, flat	11. type	boxed, exposed, all-inclusive
6. age	old, young, ancient	12. purpose	cooking, sleeping, teaching

Examples:

They met two tall, middle-aged Cuban men.

Docked there were three smallish, ancient, weather-beaten, wooden ships.

The bread was cold, round, and flecked with tiny pieces of cheese.

In our second example, we broke a "rule." You can see that mostly, however, we stuck with the order. But as we see with the second sentence, it's more logical for ancient to come just before weather-beaten. Which is a good example of wisely breaking the rules.

Appendix B
Tense, Type, and Mood
(from Chapter 20)

The information in this Appendix is derived partly from the following websites:

- Shrives, Craig. "Mood in Grammar," Grammar Monster, https://www.grammar-monster.com/glossary/mood.htm (accessed Aug. 1, 2023).
- Ellis, Matt. "Verb Tenses Explained, With Examples," Grammarly, May 10, 2023, https://www.grammarly.com/blog/verb-tenses/ (accessed Aug. 1, 2023).

The three types of *tenses*:

1. Present
2. Past
3. Future

Each *type* of tense may be:

1. simple (conveying present action)
2. perfect (conveying a past or future action)
3. continuous (conveys what is happening right now)

4. perfect continuous (conveys what has happened in the past and is still happening)

The *moods* of each tense show what is possible, or hypothetical:

1. indicative (states, asks, or denies a fact)
2. subjunctive (contrary-to-fact and hypothetical statements)
3. imperative (requests and commands)

Short examples of each are helpful and placed below. A writer has many tools in her or his toolbox! Note that these are fairly simple examples, which will work most of the time, but for more complicated constructions, more study may be warranted.

Tense (when action occurs)	Type	Mood	Sentence Example
Present	Simple	Indicative	Susan eats a tomato sandwich to satisfy her hunger.
		Subjunctive	If Susan eats a tomato sandwich her hunger will be satisfied.
		Imperative	*Susan, eat a tomato sandwich to satisfy your hunger.*
	Perfect	Indicative	Susan has eaten a tomato sandwich to satisfy her hunger.
		Subjunctive	If Susan has eaten a tomato sandwich her hunger will be satisfied.
		Imperative	*Doesn't typically exist in English.*
	Continuous	Indicative	Susan is eating a tomato sandwich to satisfy her hunger.
		Subjunctive	If Susan is eating a tomato sandwich, her hunger will be satisfied.
		Imperative	*Doesn't typically exist in English.*
	Perfect Continuous	Indicative	Susan has been eating a tomato sandwich to satisfy her hunger.
		Subjunctive	If Susan has been eating a tomato sandwich her hunger will be satisfied.
		Imperative	*Doesn't typically exist in English.*

Past	Simple	Indicative	Susan ate a tomato sandwich to satisfy her hunger.
		Subjunctive	If Susan ate a tomato sandwich, her hunger would be satisfied.
		Imperative	*Doesn't typically exist in English.*
	Perfect	Indicative	Susan had eaten a tomato sandwich which satisfied her hunger.
		Subjunctive	If Susan had eaten a tomato sandwich, her hunger would be satisfied.
		Imperative	*Doesn't typically exist in English.*
	Continuous	Indicative	Susan was eating a tomato sandwich satisfying her hunger.
		Subjunctive	If Susan was eating a tomato sandwich, her hunger would be satisfied.
		Imperative	*Doesn't typically exist in English.*
	Perfect Continuous	Indicative	Susan had been eating a tomato sandwich to satisfy her hunger.
		Subjunctive	If Susan had been eating a tomato sandwich, her hunger would be satisfied.
		Imperative	*Doesn't typically exist in English.*

Future	Simple	Indicative	Susan will eat a tomato sandwich to satisfy her hunger.
		Subjunctive	If Susan will eat a tomato sandwich, then she will satisfy her hunger.
		Imperative	Susan may eat a tomato sandwich to satisfy her hunger.
	Perfect	Indicative	Susan will have eaten a tomato sandwich to satisfy her hunger before you have time to ask her out to dinner.
		Subjunctive	If Susan will have eaten a tomato sandwich, her hunger would be satisfied.
		Imperative	*Doesn't typically exist in English.*
	Continuous	Indicative	Susan will be eating a tomato sandwich to satisfy her hunger.
		Subjunctive	If Susan will be eating a tomato sandwich, her hunger will be satisfied.
		Imperative	*Doesn't typically exist in English.*
	Perfect Continuous	Indicative	Susan will have been eating a tomato sandwich longer than anyone at her meeting.
		Subjunctive	By the time her meeting is over, Susan will have been eating a tomato sandwich to satisfy her hunger longer than anyone.
		Imperative	*Doesn't typically exist in English.*

Appendix C
Words and Phrases to Avoid, or Limit, in Your Writing
(Usually Unnecessary Words)
(From Chapter 21)

This information for this Appendix is derived from the following websites:

- Nancy Schnoebelen Imbs, "Improve Your Writing: Avoid These 10 Unnecessary Words," April 30, 2020, https://www.asaporg.com/efficiency-skills/improve-your-writing-avoid-these-10-unnecessary-words (accessed Aug. 1, 2023).

- Laura Mondragón, "70 Wordy and Redundant Phrases to Avoid in Your Writing," The Writing Cooperative, Oct. 22, 2019, https://writingcooperative.com/70-wordy-and-redun dant-phrases-to-avoid-in-your writing-f8f022b05f86 (accessed Aug. 1, 2023)

This is not a comprehensive list but can provide a feel, or pattern, of what you should do if your word or phrase is not directly listed here.

Words to avoid, or limit, in your writing

This list is derived from: "Improve Your Writing: Avoid These 10 Unnecessary Words."

Really: Although typically used to convey emphasis, it is weak in this regard.

Very: It is also used to convey emphasis, but is also quite weak in this regard.

Things: Nondescriptive word that is usually unclear; it puts the burden on the reader to figure out what is trying to be conveyed.

That: Sometimes this word has legitimate uses, but it is often not necessary and is essentially just filler. If the sentence still makes sense if taken out, then take it out.

So: This is a filler word and should often be deleted. Yet it is used in conversation, so it may be appropriate to use in dialogue, but use sparingly.

Actually: This word typically adds no real value and can be deleted. Even if in dialogue, the best use is often when the person is making a sarcastic remark: "Can you believe it? John actually took out the trash." Use sparingly, though.

Literally: This word is similar to actually and again adds no real value and can typically be deleted. Again, it could be used sparingly in dialogue.

Was/is/are/am: These words are forms of to be and quite often convey passive voice. When possible, convert these to active voice, which is typically more engaging to your readers. The sentence: *The letter was typed yesterday and you should receive it tomorrow* . . . could just as easily be written: *The letter, typed yesterday, should be received tomorrow.*

Just: This word is often overused and is unnecessary in most circumstances. There may be a few times when you will want to use it for emphasis, but use it sparingly; if not, it is simply ineffective.

Some: This word lacks clarity and puts the onus on the reader to understand how many items you mean. For example: *You will receive some of those documents today.* . . . could be conveyed better as: *You will receive two of those documents today.*

Other words that lack clarity and are mostly just filler words: *frankly, honestly, truthfully, quite, somewhat, seems, utterly, practically, basically, rather.* Yet these can be used in dialogue as people do say them quite often. But use them sparingly; then they can have impact. If used too often, they become mere filler words.

Wordy phrases to avoid (the choice in italics is almost always a better use):

This next list is derived from "70 Wordy and Redundant Phrases to Avoid in Your Writing."

in terms of; replace with: *regarding*

at the present time; replace with: *now*

is able to; replace with: *can*

in the near future; replace with: *soon* (or provide a specific time)

the fact that; replace with: *that*

despite the fact that; replace with: *although*

the reason why is that; replace with: *because*

be aware of the fact that; replace with: *note*

the fact that it doesn't have; replace with: *its lack of*

in light of the fact that; replace with: *considering*

less than great: replace with: *subpar*

comes equipped with; replace with: *includes*

it's important to note that; replace with: *notably*

in the direction of; replace with *toward*

make a choice; replace with: *choose* (or *decide*)

the truth is that; replace with: *nothing*; delete these words entirely!

Unnecessary prepositions

beat out; instead say: *beat*

start off; instead say: *start*

match up; instead say: match

head up; just say: *head*

finish up; just say: *finish*

enter into; just say: *enter*

exit out of; instead: *exit*

depart from; instead: *depart*

permeate through; just say: *permeate*

escape from; just say: *escape*

flee from; far better: *flee*

orbit around; far better: *orbit*

clean up; instead say: *clean*

shout out: instead say: *shout*

jump up; always just say: *jump*

sit down; always just say: *sit* (when one sits, of course, it is always a downward movement)

Redundant phrases

as per: instead say: *per*

share the same; instead say: *share*

both agree; instead say: *agree*

laptop computer; just say: *laptop*

cheaper price; just say: *cheaper* (or *lower price*)

on sale for a discounted rate; just say: *on sale* (or *discounted*)

debut of a new product; just say: *product debut*

collide into each other; just say: *collide*

crammed close together: just say: *crammed*

insist adamantly; instead say: *insist*

tragically sad; instead say: *tragic*

tall skyscraper; instead: *skyscraper*

urban city; instead: *city*

a little bit; just say: *a bit (or a little)*

small bits; just say: *bits*

hotter temperature; just say: *hotter (or higher temperature)*

colder temperature; just say: *colder (or lower temperature)*

once used to do; instead say: *did (or used to)*

used to at one time; instead: *used to*

used to in the past; just say: *used to*

deceptive lie; just say: *lie* (lies are always, of course, deceptive)

dark, black sky: just say: *black sky*

scrutinize very carefully; just say: *scrutinize*

wander around aimlessly; just say: *wander (or roam)*

Appendix D
Tips on How to Set Writing Goals
(From Chapter 23)

5 Tips to Help Set Writing Goals

If you want to write that novel or self-help book you've always wanted to put into print, you need more than just a plan. It's recommended that you outline the steps you'll take to achieve it. (Yes, we remember the "pantser" section earlier in the book. You may write that way. But if you're a newer writer or writing a nonfiction book, it's highly recommended to create an outline in some way similar to below.)

Additional ideas in this appendix were derived from the following website:

- MasterClass, "5 Tips for Setting Achievable Writing Goals," MasterClass, November 12, 2021, https://www.masterclass.com/articles/tips-for-setting-achievable-writing-goals (accessed Aug. 1, 2023).

1. Create realistic goals

Set realistic writing goals that seem ideal for you. Don't compare yourself to what others are doing. Their circumstances are not the same as yours, so don't compare your number of words per day to theirs. *As long as you establish daily habits that propel you forward toward your goal and you feel comfortable with them, you have a realistic goal.* Masterclass has provided the following goals that many writers have developed for themselves. Give them a try. If you feel they are too aggressive, cut back. If you feel they are too lax, increase the pace of your work. It's all about you, your lifestyle, your responsibilities. Tailor to those, but keep moving forward.

Potential goals:

- Write 1,500 words every day
- Write for three hours every day at a scheduled time
- Finish one chapter each week
- Practice morning journaling

2. Create measurable goals

Don't set vague goals. Create goals that are trackable and can be checked off as your go. *Keep them small but measurable so you can visually see yourself moving forward by checking them off as you accomplish them.* That will keep your momentum going and also help you establish good daily writing habits.

Have an end goal in mind and put a date on it. Then break that down into measurable bite-size goals you can accomplish each day. Then, simply by being consistent, you will achieve what in the beginning seemed insurmountable. Even if you don't complete all you had planned, still, celebrate! Why? You are now so much closer to your main goal than you were when you set those goals.

3. Track your progress (through use of a calendar)

One of the easiest ways to track your progress is by using a calendar. *Set daily goals and then check off what you have accomplished each day.* You may also want to keep a journal so you can keep track of how well things are going and, conversely, which areas are proving challenging. Then you know how to adjust and reset your goals. Maybe your word count is too aggressive. No problem. If you see how many words you've been able to achieve, say, in the last fourteen days, then revise, reset, and continue on. That is not failure, that is resetting for success.

4. Be accountable

The goals you set should be a high priority for you. This is your way of making yourself accountable and learning time management. Your journal will help you know the *pace* you should be following, the *time of day* that works best for you, and where is the *best place* for you to write. In the beginning, you can adjust these areas as you figure out what works best. *But then, once you've figured out those optimal choices, be accountable and stick with them.* That's how you become a writer. Take yourself and your craft seriously.

5. Find your motivation

You have your reasons for becoming an author. Don't compare yourself to others. *Compare yourself to the goals you have set. Reward yourself!* When you reach a certain number of days *being successful with your goals, treat yourself in some way.* Make it fun! Maybe when you reach a certain word count, take a day off and have a blast doing something you like to do. Then come back the next day with more rejuvenated enthusiasm.

If you need more motivation, attend a writers' conference (there are many), find a podcast that you identify with (there are tons), or read other writers' blogs or watch their vlogs (again, many). Doing these things will help you feel you're not alone, give you great ideas for how to go about the craft, and help stimulate your thought processes for what you're writing about as well.

Being a writer is not an easy path, but it doesn't have to be an arduous, lonely one. It can be full of life, vitality, and inspiration.

Appendix E
Wonderful Writing Resources*

Ackerman, Angela and Becca Puglisi: *The Emotion Thesaurus: A Writer's Guide to Character Expression,* 2nd Ed., Writers for Writers: 2019.

Browne, Renni and Dave King: *Self-Editing for Fiction Writers: How to Edit Yourself into Print,* 2nd Ed., Harper Collins, New York, NY: 2004.

Chicago Manual of Style: The Essential Guide for Writers, Editors, and Publishers, 17th Ed., University of Chicago Press, Chicago, IL, 2017.

Clark, Roy Peter: *Writing Tools: 50 Essential Strategies for Every Writer,* Little, Brown and Company, Boston, MA, 2006.

Deardon, Amy: *The Story Template: Conquer Writer's Block Using the Universal Structure of Story,* Taegais Publishing, Sykesville, MD, 2011.

Dockens, Randy C. and Robert Irvin: *Mastering the ABCs of Excellent Self-Editing: Framing Your Colorful Masterpiece to Keep Readers Engaged,* Clovercroft Publishing, Franklin, TN, 2023.

King, Stephen, *On Writing: A Memoir of the Craft,* Simon & Schuster Inc., New York, NY, 2000.

Strunk Jr., William and E. B. White: *The Elements of Style,* 4th Ed., 2023.

Zinsser, William: *On Writing Well: The Classic Guide to Writing Nonfiction,* Collins, New York, NY, 2016.

* There are dozens if not hundreds of excellent books on developing the craft of writing and writing well. This list is far from exhaustive, and we by no means mean to imply these are the best. They are just some of our favorites.

Endnotes

1. Jim Bishop, *The Day Christ Died* (New York: Harper Collins Publishers, 1957, 1977), p. 185.

2. "Arranging Multiple Adjectives: The Blue Book of Grammar and Punctuation," Grammarbook.com, 2023, https://www.grammarbook.com/ blog/commas/arranging-multiple-adjectives/ (accessed Aug. 1, 2023).

3. Cambridge Dictionary, "Order of Adjectives," English Grammar Today, https://dictionary.cambridge.org/us/grammar/british-grammar/adjectives-order (accessed Aug. 1, 2023).

4. *Chicago Manual of Style, 15th Edition* (Chicago, London: University of Chicago Press, 2003), p. 147.

5. *Chicago Manual of Style, 15th Edition,* pp. 290, 291.

6. Ibid.

7. John Lennon, Paul McCartney, "Paperback Writer," The Beatles (EMI: London, May 1966). The song was released as a single and not on any Beatles album.

8. Amy Deardon, *The Story Template: Conquer Writer's Block Using the Universal Structure of Story* (Taegais Publishing), 2017.

9. C.S. Lewis, *The Lion, the Witch, and the Wardrobe* (New York: HarperCollins, 2008).

10. Deardon, *The Story Template,* pp. 71-73.

11. Stephen King, *On Writing: A Memoir of the Craft* (New York: Simon & Schuster's Pocket Books, 2000), pp. 139, 140, 142.

12. Craig Shrives, "Mood in Grammar," Grammar Monster, https://www. grammar-monster.com/glossary/mood.htm(accessed Aug. 1, 2023).

13. Matt Ellis, "Verb Tenses Explained, With Examples," Grammarly, May 10, 2023, https://www.grammarly.com/blog/verb-tenses/ (accessed Aug. 1, 2023).

14. Nancy Schnoebelen, "Improve Your Writing: Avoid These 10 Unnecessary Words," April 30, 2020, https://www.asaporg.com/efficiency-skills/improve-your-writing-avoid-these-10-unnecessary-words (accessed Aug. 1, 2023).

15. Laura Mondragón, "70 Wordy and Redundant Phrases to Avoid in Your Writing," The Writing Cooperative, Oct. 22, 2019, https://writing-cooperative.com/70-wordy-and-redundant-phrases-to-avoid-in-your-writing-f8f022b05f86 (accessed Aug. 1, 2023).

16. Kathy Gates, "What Are Plotters And Pantsers? Hint: J.K. Rowling Is One and Stephen King Is the Other," AMREADING, September 18, 2018, https://www.amreading.com/2016/09/18/what-are-plotters-and-pantsers-hint-j-k-rowling-is-one-and-stephen-king-is-the-other/ (accessed Aug. 1, 2023).

17. Ibid.

18. Ibid.

19. King, *On Writing: A Memoir of the Craft*, pp. 159, 160.

20. Agatha Christie, *And Then There Were None* (Penguin Group, USA; Agatha Christie Limited; all rights reserved, 1939). From Author's Note to a later published edition. Christie first wrote of the difficulty of writing the novel that only she would know in *An Autobiography*.

21. Barnaby Conrad and Monte Schultz, eds., *Snoopy's Guide to the Writing Life* (Cincinnati: Writer's Digest Books, 2002), p. 30.

22. William Zinsser, *On Writing Well: The Classic Guide to Writing Nonfiction* (New York, London: Harper Perennial, 1976, 2006), p. 20.

23. Zinsser, *On Writing Well*, p. 23.

24. MasterClass, "5 Tips for Setting Achievable Writing Goals," MasterClass, November 12, 2021, https://www.masterclass.com/articles/tips-for-setting-achievable-writing-goals (accessed Aug. 1, 2023).

About the Authors

Randy is an author of fiction with three series of futuristic fiction (The Coded Message Trilogy, Stele Prophecy Pentalogy, and Erabon Prophecy Trilogy) and one of biblical fiction (The Adversary Chronicles), but has written nonfiction as well (*Why Is a Gentile World Tied to a Jewish Timeline? The Question Everyone Should Ask*). Other books in both types of work are also planned. He describes his books as futuristic with a science fiction feel and a Christian perspective. He has a doctorate in both pharmacokinetics (how drugs work in the body) and in biblical prophecy. His books are a way to bring both science and biblical aspects together in a different, unique, and fun way with a combination of mystery, intrigue, and romance in a futuristic setting with an overlay of just enough of a scientific touch to make each story feel realistic. You can find out more about his works at his author website: www.RandyDockens.com.

This book is an endeavor to pay forward many of the things he has learned on his writing journey so that others can start, learn, or refresh what they know but may have forgotten about the different aspects of what goes into good writing. It is hoped that the elements in this book will help those who read it develop a methodical approach to creating habits of good writing that can enhance one's artful style of writing no matter the genre.

Robert has been a professional writer and editor for most of his adult life.  He started in journalism and worked in all levels of newspaper reporting and editing, from the proverbial cub reporter to bureau chief, night city desk editor, and newsroom editor. He has written award-winning pieces for several magazines. In 2005 he chose publishing and worked for Standard Publishing (Cincinnati) until 2011, then going independent. He does the majority of his work with Christian Book Services. He has ghostwritten long portions of books for authors and entire books for a World War II veteran's memoirs (written 2013-2015 at age 89-91!) and a former NFL quarterback's story of mentoring his high school football star son.

Robert has edited virtually every type of book, from business to novels to theology to sports to abuse survival stories, and much more. His credits includes scores of books. He has spoken at or served as faculty at various writing conferences.

He enjoys family, the outdoors, running, bad golf (like many, he has the bug, which just won't go away), a heated game of Scrabble, virtually any sport, and reading any book that even remotely interests him. He and wife Joan have four children.

To complete your vivid and colorful story, order our companion book on excellent self-editing.

Writing and self-editing are intricately connected, but they are definitely two separate events. This book gets you to your first draft, the colorful masterpiece you have created. It's not ready for prime time, though. You need to frame your masterpiece so your readers will see it as the powerful story you know it to be. Our book on self-editing will help you do just that.

Our second book in this short series will cover various self-editing techniques to help make your writing something readers will enjoy. It will greatly assist you with the artistic side of editing so that what is inside of you—your writing style, your brand—will shine through.

As with this one, our self-editing book is an easy-to-enjoy manual written in a unique alphabetical style, filled with tips and extra-information boxes at the end of each chapter, and has several helpful additions following the final chapter. What we share will greatly enhance your masterpiece whether it is fiction or nonfiction writing.

Made in the USA
Middletown, DE
20 May 2024